Daddy —
For you when you
get nostalgic!
Love,
Kathleen

Ghosts Along the Mississippi

Ghosts along

MISSI

AN ESSAY IN THE POETIC INTERPRETATION

the

OF LOUISIANA'S PLANTATION ARCHITECTURE

BY

Clarence John Laughlin

ONE HUNDRED PHOTOGRAPHS BY THE AUTHOR

BONANZA BOOKS, NEW YORK

(N)

This edition published by Bonanza Books, a division of Crown Publishers, Inc., by arrangement with the author Clarence John Laughlin.

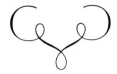

Some hang above the tombs,
Some weep in empty rooms,
I, when the iris blooms,
    Remember.

—MARY COLERIDGE

The night comes on:
You wait and listen . . .
To all these ghosts of change.
And they are you.

—CONRAD AIKEN (FROM "THE CLOISTERS")

Printed in the United States of America

ILLUSTRATIONS

List of Louisiana Plantation Houses Appearing in This Book

AFTON VILLA: near St. Francisville. Open to the public. (Plates 74-76)

ASHLAND: near Geismar. On East River Road. Restoration again in progress. (Plates 60-63)

AUSTERLITZ: near New Roads. (Plate 31)

BEAUREGARD, RENÉ: next to Battlefield of New Orleans, Chalmette National Historical Park. The house has now been restored, and its second floor houses a battle museum. Open to the public. (Plate 55)

BELLE ALLIANCE: near Belle Rose. On East Bayou Lafourche Road. (Plate 64)

BELLECHASSE: near Belle Chasse. On West River Road. (Plate 65)

BELLE GROVE: was near White Castle. Destroyed by fire in 1952. (Plates 84-92)

BELLE HÉLÈNE: *see* Ashland Plantation.

BOCAGE: near Burnside. On East River Road. Now completely restored. (Plate 54)

BRINGIER HOUSE, THE: *see* Tezcuco.

BURNSIDE: *see* The Houmas House.

CHATEAU DES FLEURS: was on Angela Avenue in New Orleans. (Plates 25-26)

CHRÉTIEN POINT: near Sunset. (Plates 37-39)

CONRAD PLACE, THE: *see* The Cottage.

COTTAGE, THE: was near Baton Rouge. Destroyed by fire in 1960. (Plates 32-33)

EVERGREEN: near Edgard. On West River Road. (Plates 35-36)

GREENWOOD: near St. Francisville. Destroyed by fire in 1960. (Plates 42-44)

HERMITAGE, THE: near Darrow. On East River Road. (Plate 41)

HOUMAS HOUSE, THE: near Burnside. On East River Road. (Plates 56-59)

LABATUT: near Labarre. (Plates 19-20)

LINWOOD: was near Burnside. (Plate 40)

LIVE OAK: near Bains. (Plate 29)

MADEWOOD: near Napoleonville. On East Bayou Lafourche Road. (Plates 66-68)

MYRTLES, THE: near St. Francisville. Open to the public. (Plate 78)

OAK ALLEY: near Vacherie. On West River Road. Open to the public. (Plates 50-53)

OAK LAWN: near Baldwin. (Plate 45)

OAKLEY: near St. Francisville. The house has now been restored as an Audubon shrine. The grounds, sheltering again the birds Audubon loved, are known as Audubon Memorial State Park. Open to the public. (Plates 27-28)

ORANGE GROVE: was near Braithwaite. (Plate 77)

ORMOND: near Destrehan. On East River Road. (Plates 12-13)

PARLANGE: near New Roads. (Plates 14-16)

PINE ALLEY: was near St. Martinville. (Plate 34)

RIENZI: near Thibodaux. On East Bayou Lafourche Road. (Plate 22)

ROSEDOWN: near St. Francisville. (Plates 46-49)

SAN FRANCISCO: near Garyville. On East River Road. Since 1954 has been the home of Mr. and Mrs. Clark Thompson, who have restored its original beauty. Open to the public. (Plates 79-81)

TEZCUCO: near Burnside. On East River Road. Open to the public. (Plates 82-83)

TRÉPAGNIER: near south side of Bonnet Carré Spillway. On East River Road. Demolished in 1954. (Plate 11)

UNCLE SAM: was near Convent. Demolished in 1940. (Plates 69-73)

VERSAILLES: was near Battlefield of New Orleans. Destroyed in 1876. (Plate 24)

VOISIN: near Reserve. On East River Road. (Plates 17-18)

WAVERLY: near Bains. (Plate 30)

WOODLAWN: was near Napoleonville. (Plates 93-99)

ZENON-TRUDEAU: near Convent. On East River Road. In ruins. (Plate 23)

PROLOGUE

THIS book will attempt to present the evolution of Louisiana plantation culture in terms of the contrast, and the adhesion, of two subtly related, yet unlike, elements—that which may roughly be called historico-architectural, and that which pulsates around poetic vision. Nearly equal emphasis will be given the architectural and the poetic aspects of the material. Ordinarily, this might be considered a rather difficult, if not impossible, combination. Perhaps it can be demonstrated that rather than being mutually exclusive, the two elements may actually supplement and strengthen one another.

From the historical and architectural facts (as they are known) regarding the erection of the plantation houses we must borrow the bones of our structure—this skeleton, however, can assume no significant or final reality till it is clothed in the flesh of poetic perception. By this is not meant merely superficial romanticism. The method of poetry is to abstract symbols from the stuff of living experience; to embody these symbols not only in emotive language, but, by means of the creative use of these symbols, to subtly penetrate beyond the tough outer skin of appearances, and give us a reality which is not only complexly sweetened or embittered by the perceiving mind, but *more extensive in time* than that reality which is immediately apprehensible; since now elements of the past and of the future play equal parts with that of the present. In the superior reality of poetic vision we enter a plane where symbols have a life of their own; and here perhaps we transcend, temporarily and incompletely, the limitations which time, or rather, our three-dimensional realization of time, places upon us.

In any such brief account of the nature of Louisiana plantation culture as this, the use of a poetic approach is made essential by the very nature of the culture itself; by the presence in it of factors not wholly economic; and by the marked individual character of the houses which gave it expression. No assemblage of facts and figures will ever give us the complete reality of the transient loveliness of so fleeting a thing, for instance, as the language of the body—a lithe movement, the nameless luminescence of an eye, the wordless implications of a smile, or the grace of a flower in the wind. Similarly, no coldly correct presentation of the exact dimensions of a wall or of a column, or even measured drawings of an entire building, can ever give us the total reality a house has (if it *is* a good house) as an *entity*. Its special kind of life can never be conveyed to us wholly by any mass of technical details, however painstaking—only the eye of the imagination can relate all the many elements which go to make up the house as an organic whole. The intangible thing that can be called the life of a house is treated somewhat further in Part II of this Prologue.

For the moment, it shall suffice to say that a fundamental purpose of this book is to present— by means of the opposition, and the subtle relationships, of the two elements outlined above —the magic and enigma of old houses, which qualities the houses of old Louisiana possess in a peculiarly individual way, and to an extent unequalled, perhaps, in the United States. The contrast and the interweaving of the two perspectives shall, of course, be carried into the pictures, in many of which this writer has definitely attempted to transcend the customary recording usage of the camera. Not only can the imagination give us something more than any exact set of plans and specifications, but its creative power can at times be projected, despite popular misconceptions to the contrary, through the searching eye of the camera's lens.

Since the camera is a machine only when it is used mechanically—it is possible to discover and present through it poetic and psychological reality as well as "record" reality—when it is used imaginatively. But whatever special imaginative quality the pictures in this book may have, it is, the reader may be assured, a direct outgrowth of the intrinsic nature of the material; an expression, through the camera, of the mysterious and moving quality which the best of the old houses of Louisiana seem to possess in a way particularly their own, setting them apart from all other old houses of the country. The innate character of this special quality is such that it lifts the houses far above the merely picturesque or pretty, while being, at the same time, so subtly and insiduously lovely as to defy analysis in terms of the type of romanticism Hollywood has so largely fostered in our time. Such analysis as it is possible to make in words will be found in the second portion of this Prologue.

This book, however, has still another basic purpose. It is to reveal Louisiana as not merely one of the most important of the regional sources of our American architectural heritage—but as one of the first native germinal grounds of modern architecture. This may seem a bit presumptuous or unfounded. But we must not assume that Louisiana plantation architecture derives its importance to the modern mind simply from its historic values on the one hand; nor from its romantic associations, or genuinely poetic connotations, on the other. Rather, it can be shown that in the lower Mississippi valley, for the first time in 19th century America, some houses arose which were actually designed in terms of the materials used, and the climate. These houses, therefore, should have meaning even to those not greatly interested in romantic legend or antiquarian research.

Which leaves us with but one more observation to offer on the general plan of the book. It will be noted that in order to show more clearly the evolution of the Louisiana houses, the pictures and notes have been arranged, with but few exceptions (notably Woodlawn), in a roughly chronological order. This should be of help to those more historically minded.

I

THE HISTORICO-ARCHITECTURAL PERSPECTIVE

THE evolution of the plantation culture of the lower Mississippi valley—which, during the early and middle years of the nineteenth century, put forth an architectural efflorescence amazing both for its vigor and its feeling for materials—is embedded in a nexus of historical, architectural, and sociological factors. It might be well to review some of these shortly.

The first evidence of the growth, which was to flower into the greatest architectural expression in the entire central United States, began simply enough in 1726 in such a "raised cottage" as Madame John's Legacy. Originally merely a planter's simple structure in the wilderness, it was later enveloped by the wealthy and turbulent French town that became the heart of New Orleans. Derived directly from Madame John's Legacy were such structures as we see in Plates 11, 12, 13, 14 and 17—structures with cement-covered brick walls and columns below; the upper level of wood and brick with their frontal walls composed of beams packed between with earth and bricks; while the colonettes were of hand carved cypress. The roofs were long-sloped and always of shingles; cypress being usually used for the gutters. This was the Colonial period in Louisiana architecture.

In connection with this period, there has been a good deal of conjecture, as to the nature, and the extent, of the influence of 18th century West Indian rural architecture on the development of the Louisiana plantation houses. And while, as in the case of Melrose Plantation, this influence undoubtedly made itself felt—it does not seem, to this writer, ever to have attained a predominant part; remaining, rather, but one factor in a synthesis whose final coloring, in the Louisiana Colonial style, attained indigenousness. Obviously enough, of course, West Indian influence played no part in the grand style which was to follow.

That following style, in 1825, evidenced itself in such a structure as The Cottage (The Conrad Place) (Plate 32)—where are many of the most distinctive features of what, for lack of a better term, could be called Louisiana (or Creole) Classic style, which appeared here in one of its earliest instances. This style was made up of Greek Revival and, sometimes, Georgian influences (with the former far more important), but dominated by characteristics endemic to Louisiana. Thus it represented a unique combination of factors. In the typical example of this style can be found great rounded brick columns surrounding the main body of the house (the columns modified Tuscan in character, usually, rather than Doric as they are often called); wide encircling galleries spreading from the walls to the columns; a hipped and dormered roof; the floor plan being a simple one—a wide central hall flanked, usually, by four rooms. The same plan was commonly repeated on the second floor. Uncle Sam Plantation (Plates 69 and 70), and Oak Alley Plantation (Plates 50 and 51) are examples of such a proto-type as the Conrad Place.

It was, then, during the 1820's when Greek Revival first appeared to any great extent in Louisiana; by 1840 its influence was predominant—though curiously modified and acclimatized, in many cases, by certain characteristics of the style which had preceded it; and especially, by the nature of the materials used in Louisiana—since these continued the same—so that, eventually, Greek Revival in Louisiana acquired so markedly a different flavor from Greek Revival in the north that it became, essentially, an element in a separate style—the style which, as previously mentioned, can be called Louisiana or Creole Classic. Even in those Louisiana houses where, for special reasons, Greek Revival did not depart so widely from examples elsewhere in the United States, the difference in flavor was still observable. (Compare, for instance, the Belding House in Troy, New York—Plate LXXV in Talbot Hamlin's "Greek Revival Architecture in America"—with Madewood Plantation, Plate 66 in this book.)

In the 1850's the taste of the planters experienced some pronounced modifications when Victorianism invaded Louisiana, producing such strange and fantastic houses as the pseudo-Gothic of Afton Villa (Plate 74) and the "steamboat" Gothic of San Francisco Plantation (Plate 79).

The evolution of Louisiana plantation architecture unfolded, finally (in 1857), into such a huge structure as Belle Grove (see Plates 84 to 90), where much of the feeling of the Louisiana classic style had been lost in importations from Europe, in Greek Revival via the Palladian villas of north Italy. However, even Belle Grove differed widely in a number of respects from such a house as Rattle and Snap in Tennessee (see Plate LXVI in Talbot Hamlin's *Greek Revival Architecture in America*) to which house, in this country, it was most closely related.

It should here be indicated that the best architectural expressions of Louisiana plantation culture represent more than merely adaptations of French provincial originals, on the one hand;

or classic derivations, on the other—that they, in fact, embodied something peculiar to the lower Mississippi valley. It may be said correlatively that there is in many of them an architectural feeling as close to being truly indigenous as anything that can be found throughout the United States of the 19th century—not even omitting New England.

The fundamental physical factors behind the development of the indigenous style which can be called Louisiana or Creole were: (a) the semi-tropic climatic conditions of Louisiana (with their special demands because of the heavy rainfall and the high humidity); (b) the extensive use of purely local materials for building, and the rooting of the style in the nature of these materials. Even in cases where "derived" architectural feeling was pronounced the use of local materials gave the derivations a special character.

One of the basic facts that must be remembered in any discussion of materials, is that there are no stone quarries anywhere in Louisiana. All stone, when it was used, (which was seldom) had to be brought from far away on ships—sometimes New England, sometimes even Europe. South Louisiana was isolated from the rest of the United States by its impassable swamps, by distance, by bad roads, and had no effective communication save by sea and river. And beneath the rich deep alluvial soil of south Louisiana no rock could be struck, no matter how deeply piles were driven.

On the other hand slave labor was cheap and there was the great river with its inexhaustible banks of clay. Bricks were manufactured on a huge scale, often right on the spot while construction was taking place. And the bricks were bonded with a mortar of great tenacity—the exact nature of whose composition seems lost—but, even today, modern wrecking crews have great difficulty dismantling the brick walls of some of the old houses. Meanwhile, in the swamps, grew the funereal and gigantic water-loving cypresses. Their wood, in the form of huge beams, became a cheap, and ideal material for large portions of the great houses because of its easy workability, and more importantly, its damp-resistant properties.

Unlike New Orleans, where iron was used in great profusion, very little iron appeared on any of the plantation structures (save on a few of those more nearly non-indigenous in feeling, as for instance, Belle Grove); the railings of the broad galleries were usually of cypress wood. And no stone columns ever appeared—the columns were invariably of plastered brick, or of wood, with the former predominating. The capitals for the columns, too, were often of plastered brick, sometimes cypress wood (as is the case, surprisingly, of Belle Grove whose hand-carved capitals, applied in four sections around the brick cores of the pillars, have withstood weathering even better than the plastered brick), and, more rarely, of cast iron. There is only one instance known to this writer where any of the Louisiana houses had capitals composed of materials other than those mentioned—the capitals of Woodlawn Plantation (Plates 93 to 99) were of stone, but on plastered brick columns.

The plaster for the columns was, at times, tinted; though quite frequently it was left to acquire a soft and luminous whiteness—which together with the soft lines and textures of the walls, resulted in a beautiful integration of tone and form—helped, of course, by the usually simple and severe lines of the wooden cornices, door and window frames, and by the effective opposition of the textures of the cypress wood with the plastered surfaces. When tints were used (particularly on the interior walls) they were of a softness and subtlety that were exquisite, and gave the houses a warmth quite beyond words.

Taking into account all the factors indicated above—it cannot be too strongly stressed that in terms of the materials *then* available, in terms of the special psychological needs of the people of *that* time and place, and the particular climatic demands of south Louisiana—the best of the plantation houses were as *functional* as anything we have today. Indeed, in looking at such houses as Chrétien Point, Uncle Sam, Oak Alley, as well as at some of the simple slave cabins—we must feel that here are structures actually designed so purely and directly in terms of the intrinsic character of cypress wood and the plastic capacities of plastered brick—and so delicately integrated by line and tint—that the design seems to have grown, inevitably and profoundly, from their substance. And it is then we realize how closely this achievement relates them to one of the fundamental concerns of the modern architect—feeling for the innate qualities of materials —giving them thus a far from unimportant relationship to contemporary architecture.

The plan of a typical Louisiana plantation became this: near the river would be the main house (usually led up to by a great avenue of oaks); its pillars, for the most part, entirely surrounding the house; flanking it to either side were two *garçonnières* much smaller in size (originally, these were for the sons of a family and his friends; later, they were simply guest houses); behind the main house were normally two more structures—the plantation overseer's office, and the plantation kitchen (kept separated, in most cases, from the main house because of the danger of fire); somewhat further back were often dovecotes or pigeon houses; then the twin long lines of the slave cabins (the earlier ones of brick, the later of white-washed wood); succeeding these, the cane or cotton fields, and finally, either the cotton gin or the sugar mill.

Invariably, and symbolically, the plantation houses faced the water streams, which, in the majority of instances, meant the great Mississippi. It was the bearer of their produce, their path to the outer world, the means by which their profit and power were realized, the sentient artery which tied them to the culture of France—many of the planter's sons being educated in Europe, and much of the furniture of the great houses being imported directly into Louisiana from Paris. And like a living thing, the great river, though retained by endless man-made embankments called levees, constantly changed its course, undermining the levees, leaving behind it forgotten and cut-off segments of its convolutions that became "blind" lakes. Always it hung above the houses—threatening them with flood and destruction, yet bringing to them tangible and enormous wealth and all the things that made the art of living possible. And about its flexuous and writhing banks grew up the first and only truly non-urban and decentralized culture in the United States of the nineteenth century—for, in most respects, the plantations were entirely self-sustaining.

While beneath all this superstructure of wealth and power—their backs bowed to the unmerciful sun in the green glistening waves of the cane, in the phantasmal wispish fields of cotton —were the slaves; a reality as significant as the reality of the timeless menace and the golden beneficence of the river. In some instances, they were bred as thoughtfully and with almost as much selectivity as the cattle (since they were valuable possessions), the physically superior males being allowed to move freely among the women in spring, so that larger and healthier broods of children could be produced. In other cases, the planters treated them with genuine kindness—providing hospitals on their own plantations and sometimes, even setting them free. The most that can be said however, as a whole, was that the slave system, unlike our modern industrial system, provided its workers with constant, if wageless, employment, and usually did not let them starve. Too, there were probably many instances where personal relationships between workers and owners were better than in many cases today. But like modern Fascism the slave system denied the equality of all races; although unlike Fascism it did not channel all the energies of its workers into destruction.

The economic basis for the evolution of the plantation houses of Louisiana in the nineteenth century, was, of course, two great tides of wealth—the first from cotton (roughly 1800 to 1860);

the second from sugar (roughly 1820 to 1880). Within the framework of just a little under a century Louisiana plantation culture rose to vertiginous heights, and toppled. The decline of this culture was brought about by three factors: (1) the economic havoc wrought by the Civil War, especially by the disintegration of the slave system; (2) the later, and successive collapse of the cotton and sugar markets (upon which huge fortunes had been founded), caused by international competition; (3) the advent of industrialism and the resultant shifts in the ownership and distribution of the land, the usages of wealth, and the character of living patterns. The adverse effects of all these factors on the survival of the houses have been cumulative.

Since the beginning of this century, fire and flood, levee set-backs, the ravages of heat and dampness, and the neglect due to impoverishment, have all taken an increasing toll of the structures left from the great nineteenth century architectural blossoming. To mention only a few instances (mostly from quite recent years): Valcour Aime, Richland, and the Chateau des Fleurs—all destroyed by fire; Belair, Uncle Sam, and Chatsworth—swallowed by the river; Linwood—demolished in 1939 for the bricks contained in it; Belle Grove, Versailles, and Wood-lawn—now in utmost ruin, even though we may call the ruins beautiful.

Within a very recent period the tide has partially turned, resulting in some notable restorations, such as The Houmas House (Plate 56). However, many of the greatest, and finest, of the houses have been, long since, completely destroyed, or, as in the case of Belle Grove, have been condemned to irrevocable ruin. There is but one tragic compensation—about many of these ruins is a disturbing and mournful beauty whose magic cannot be equalled in America.

II

THE POETIC PERSPECTIVE

THE foremost symbol in the mythos of plantation culture is, probably, the river. No account, however slight, of the great houses of Louisiana, of their growth, their grandeur, and their decay, can possibly avoid mentioning the Mississippi. What pictures its history conjures! — the nights when the pioneer's tiny craft plied the stream, with its single light, perhaps a torch's flare, making a lonely eerie gleam on the waters flowing black and soundless into the savage wilderness; the days of the flatboats and the hardy brutal rivermen, bringing grain down to the mills of New Orleans; the days of the great pleasure boats of the planters (before the roads were built) with their incredible opulence; the nights of flood, with the river a blind monster gnawing at the levee; the days and nights of the river packets, loaded with cotton, the smoke, from the stacks wreathed with iron fernery, making strange fleeting patterns against a fantastically swollen and luminous moon; the slow sensual fall and rise of the chants of the Negro roustabouts pulsing to the slow contractions of the muscles of their powerful bodies, slow and powerful, dark and strong as the sweep of the river. Soundless and uncaring, creator and destroyer, the river flowed on; through the night of the magnolia, whose scent gives the very darkness a body; through the night in day of the cypress clad in moss, whose thick webs trap the light of the sun; through the days of glory and riches; the long night of war and disaster and irretrievable ruin. . . . From the lands of the north, locked in ice, the lands of the wheat field and the immeasurable prairie, the river reached in fruitful union with the lands of the south, the lands of the swamp and the cotton field, the land where the frogs sang their somnolent night songs of eternal summer. . . .

The eye, moving mentally through time and space, sees the enormous coils of the great river, the river moving thickly and powerfully to the far Gulf; the river, the stealthy tightening or loosening of whose convolutions through the course of the years, meant disaster, or wealth and fruitfulness untold to the men who hated it, who loved it, who fought it, but who could never tear their lives from its spell; to whom it brought everything they had, but from whom it could take everything away. The river, artery then pulsing still with life-blood from the cultural ganglia of Europe; the river—the broad liquid path over which their cotton, sugar and rice found the world's markets. All their great houses faced the river; all their dreams of wealth and power had to use it as their medium. And in what houses those dreams crystallized! Woodlawn, Linwood, and Parlange; Belle Grove, Belle Hélène and Bon Séjour; Houmas House and the Chateau des Fleurs; Madewood, Greenwood, Valcour Aime—what magical names are these!

Possibly the next most potent poetic source rises from the special character, the subtle beauty, of the houses themselves—particularly those which have been abandoned to time, and to which ruin has imparted a captivating, and almost eerie, quality. Any inquiry into the aesthetics of this curious poetry, however, leads us ineluctably into the attempt to analyze what may roughly be called the life of a house. That architecturally good houses have character almost in a human sense is obvious. We feel something more than this, however, when we refer vaguely to the life of a house. If the existence of a building in time could be accelerated—if, for instance, a year were to become an hour—then we should see façades wrinkle and age much as do human features—many things would seem animate which now seem lifeless. Changes in the tempo of the time-sense would reveal to us how living a thing a building is. With this concept (which shall later be extended) in mind we return once more to the specific factors that distinguish the living houses of Louisiana.

What is it, specifically, which draws us to these houses? Is it only that the tongue of an imperative melancholy speaks to us from them—the siren song, tender beyond words, of a still sensate past? Or is it not, rather, something still more complex—something allied to the nostalgic sense of the past, but even more subtle? Let us try, insofar as we can, to analyze this.

From the uncertainties of this world, this age, we turn to the only certainties—the things upon which our senses seize, however briefly; the things that delight our eyes, our ears, our skin, and to the magic aura created about these things by memory—that so carefully and subtly magnifies the emotionally significant phases of experience, and suppresses all the rest. . . . So it is that those who feel, and know, something of the mystery and magic of the old ruined houses of Louisiana find in them more than the satisfaction of mere antiquarian curiosity; find, instead, unique stimulants to vision, and to memory; and, as well, what might roughly be termed a metaphysical and poetic adventure.

The dark mystery of time, the luminous and living mystery of light—so intricately and strangely interrelated with time—the snake-brown waters of the great serpentine Mississippi— these are the chief protagonists now on the darkening stage occupied by the last structures of the doomed plantation system. They, and they alone, determine everything we see and feel. Lost in a curiously evocative pattern of light and shadow, lost in a nameless union of light and time whose intimations can never be completely phrased in words—we find again a past which, cryptically, is no longer wholly dead, a splendor no longer wholly unreal—but which lives tenuously, yet undeniably, in corroded walls, in empty and discolored chambers, in shadow entities, in the labyrinths of our blood. . . .

In houses which are old—the forms of whose very walls and pillars have taken body from the thoughts of men in a vanished time—we often sense something far more delicate, more unwordable, than the customary devices of the romanticist: the swish of a silken invisible dress on stairs once dustless, the fragrance of an unseen blossom of other years, the wraith momentarily given form in a begrimed mirror. These wordless perceptions can be due only, it seems, to something still retained in these walls; something crystallized from the energy of human emotion and the activities of human nerves. And, perhaps, it is because of this nameless life of memory and desire and, correlatively, because of a superior power of suggestion, that, for those who are sensitive, the ruined houses have a fascination far exceeding that of the intact, and inhabited structures. Within these damp vine-wrenched walls, these windows yawning from another position in time, these empty doors opening onto an age lost in space, there dwells still something unwordable, something for which the words "ghost" or "spirit" would be totally inadequate; something which is the ultimate reality from which these walls sprang, and which persists through the years; for though it came from the minds of men it has left a part of itself here. Enshadowed and made massive by the oaks, secretive and subterrane as the cypress, it remains. And that something these slow dark streams can never undermine; these fierce plant armies never breach; these sad and shadowy clouds of moss never wholly overcast.

Yes, something distilled from humanity lives in these structures yet, something condensed from time, something whose existence is as attenuated and transitory perhaps—and yet, as real —as is a shimmer on dancing water. And just as the glints on moving water represent, in a way, a fusion of light and time, so too does this secretive and innominate life that inhabits old houses, and that has risen in them because of the complex way in which the character of minds long dead has been given substance in the very structure of each building, represent an extremely subtle fusion of light and time; a fusion, it may be, that permits, briefly, a sort of hyper-seeing; a tuning of our nerves to the radiations of the nerves of those long gone beyond the direct sight of our eyes down death's endless perspective—a kind of living continuum that pierces time; that transcends, momentarily, the usual limitations placed on us by three-dimensional vision. . . . This, perhaps, is as far as our present language will allow us to carry our analysis.

And seeing these houses—perceiving, if only through the camera, some of their haunting charm—we shall be taken out of ourselves; out of our own era, with its organized madness, its frenzied concentration on multiple murder, its tempo which gives time a character wholly different from that during which the great structures of the plantation period were formed.

For, as we view the old houses of Louisiana, it is then we see, through more than our eyes alone, the beauty that comes out of time, that transcends decay; and the tenderness the years can bring, despite all their cruel metamorphoses. And this beauty carries within itself the intimation that the past can never die because it still exists, intact, on some other plane of time, around which we cannot see directly. But even if this were not true, the past cannot ever be wholly dead—for it lives in us, in our blood, in the things whose heirs we are; and the ghosts of old fears and old joys shall forever haunt us. . . .

Majestic, surely, were the great plantation houses; based upon a substratum of human exploitation, it is true; but, nevertheless, evocative of a dignity that even age cannot wholly humble; a beauty that even now, despite fire and flood and ruin, still sweeps the heart-strings with an impossible nostalgia for a time when life, for a while, had graciousness and leisure and peace. . . . This, then, is the South of the old plantation houses, the South from which, clutched by the hand of memory, something of a deathless magic eludes the blows of time. . . .

Let us turn, now, to the chronicles of some few of Louisiana's old houses whose forms, in space, have known so much of beauty; whose shapes, in time, have endured so much of joy and dismay. . . .

Ghosts Along the Mississippi

PLATE 1
ELEGY FOR MOSS LAND

THIS, the opening picture, projects, in a way, the book's whole intent, and is the result of a careful and deliberate double exposure.

In the evocative figure rising from the marsh—the earth which is unsubstantial and reflective; the inverted landscape like a swampy mirage; the plantation house, sitting in the tree of dream—is presented an image of those who seek to completely summon the past; those who fall beneath the magic spell of memory.

PLATE 2
THE MIRROR OF GRAYNESS

IN THIS quiet scene on a Louisiana bayou there is a glimpse of a mode of life completely different from the life of the cities; a mode of life contemporaneous with the rise of plantation culture, but which has managed to survive its decline. Gliding easily in their "pirogues", a local variety of dugout, the swamp people who live in the crude shacks we see, have for generations led lives devoted to hunting and fishing; lives which are poised continuously and laxly between luminous skies, the shadowy under-sky of the moss, and the smooth green sheets of the bayous. Bayous, of course, are small rivers which, because of the slight difference in elevation of the land in south Louisiana, wander irregularly and, it often seems, aimlessly.

In the distance there is visible one of Louisiana's weird dead forests; the moss converting the trees into figures of gauntness and dread. The moss, however, is not a true parasite; but, instead, what botanists call an epiphyte, taking only water from its host, yet killing the trees indirectly by shielding the leaves from the action of sunlight.

Toward the extreme left moss may be seen, hanging to dry on a line. From time immemorial, moss has been used by the early settlers to stuff their pillows and mattresses, often, too, their furniture. Today it is still used in some of the rural regions.

In this plate the true gray of the moss is conveyed—the water repeating this gray in tones more luminous and liquid.

PLATE 3
BAYOU GIRL

THE people of the Louisiana bayou and swamp country who speak, usually, a curiously modified French into which many corruptions of local origin and intonation have crept, are often known as Cajuns. They are noted for their generosity and hospitality, are fond lovers of good cooking and country dances, but can be very difficult with strangers who convey any attempt at superiority. Their sayings, their wit, their entertainments, have a peculiarly naïve folk quality which is now tending to disappear, unfortunately. But for many years, despite the great number of changes that have taken place in Louisiana's political and economic life, they have held tenaciously to their own particular customs and mannerisms.

There can be seen here one of the daughters of the Cajuns—her face revealing some of the sturdy and independent character of her people. Behind her, on the whitewashed shutter of her simple abode, the shadows of a leafless crepe myrtle tree make a dramatic and beautiful pattern.

PLATE 4

CABIN IN THE FIELDS

NONE of the great plantation houses would have been complete without their entourage of slave cabins; sometimes as many as a hundred or more of them, stretching in parallel rows behind the main house.

The very earliest slave cabins had the clay-between-posts construction characteristic of the earliest plantation houses (see Plate 11). Somewhat later, they were built of solid brick. Survivals from this period of construction are fairly rare, however. That which is seen in Plate 4 is, surprisingly, in comparatively good condition. Note the two fine solid chimneys, and how the shingled roof has been brought down well over the gallery. The house to which this cabin was attached has vanished, long since, but strangely, the cabin and a few of its companions remain, withstanding the long siege of the years, washed by the field of wild flowers, and by the heavy melting clouds in the field of the sky.

PLATE 5

BLACK AND WHITE

LATER still came the whitewashed wooden cabins, with chimneys of brick or clay. They are used to this day along many of Louisiana's bayous, and by both the whites and the Negroes.

Ida Turner is a descendant of former slaves. She remembers the tales her grandfather told of the great plantations; of the sumptuous life which was led; of the kindness, and the cruelty, but always the splendor, of life in the old days. The photographer was able to dissuade her from donning her Sunday dress for this picture, so we have the magnificent contrast of her florid dress pattern with the extreme simplicity of the wood surfaces, and their amazing textuality. The chain, used for tying the cow up nights, and the upturned tub, in which the pigs are fed, play important parts in the composition—as they do in the life of Ida Turner.

PLATE 7
WOODEN TOMBSTONE

THINGS of great strangeness—at times even unique—are still to be found in some of the old country burial grounds of Louisiana; though, of course, funeral art in rural districts never reached the heights of fantasy and elaboration attained by the justly famous cities of the dead in New Orleans. The great plantation families usually had their own private cemeteries, often on the plantation itself; though with the decline of the houses, and the collapse of the properties, many of these have been swallowed by the fields.

In addition to these, however, quite extensive, and some quite early, necropoli appeared in or near the larger towns. Many of the people of south Louisiana who trap in the swamps and fish in the numerous and everwinding streams are buried, for instance, in a strange cemetery a short distance down the river from New Orleans. Among the singular things that can be found in this place is a succession of wooden tombstones, mostly of this century, lettered in corrupt and naïve French, and carved quite carefully. One such, whose base had rotted away, has been leaned against the subtly luminous surfaces of a plastered brick tomb, for the picture shown in Plate 7. Note how the soft light delicately reveals the chalice half-hidden by the plaster of the upper tomb, and the green and luscious nature of the pattern made by the ferns growing in the crevices of the sealed opening for the coffin—life growing out of the very orifice of death.

PLATE 8

THE BOXES OF THE DEAD

THE same burial ground mentioned in the text for the preceding plate contained, till a short while past, a series of wooden boxes, lidded with glass, beneath which were curious and beautiful constructions of colored glass beads arranged on wires. The arrangement, and general feeling, of these boxes and their contents, made this cemetery probably unique in the United States, outside of Louisiana—though such boxes may be traced back to southern France. Some of the constructions resembled fantastic flowers, others were like the jewelled insects Huysmans dreamed of in "A Rebours" or Baudelaire in "Les Paradis Artificiels"; still others, from a distance, suggested vitreous eyes—the eyes, perhaps, of the poet, frozen forever by the Medusa of time.

Alas! When recently revisited, the boxes in this mysteriously beautiful place were found to have been tumbled and shattered by a chaos of untrammeled vegetation, due to lack of care during the recent war years.

PLATE 9

FROM THE MOYEN AGE

A RAISED pedimented tomb in the old cemetery of Donaldsonville, rather low in height, bears on its four upper corners, usually reserved for the conventional anthemions, four stone heads, instead. All are alike, at first glance. But lichen, encrusting the stone, has given each as much individual difference as would have the skin of four separate human faces.

Amazingly enough, the feeling of these heads strongly suggests that of some Gothic heads to be found carved in the portals of cathedrals from the fourteenth and fifteenth centuries. Only one date appears on the tomb, 1909, evidently the date of a later, additional burial—something quite common in the raised family tombs of Louisiana. The earlier dates have been lost, but it is safe to say that these heads are no earlier than 1840, and no later, probably, than 1860. It was during that period that the finest stone work in the burial grounds of Louisiana was created. No stoneworker or sculptor's name can be found; but whoever he was, his plastic sense, surely, was in mysterious alliance with the Moyen Age—the age of terror and the titanic, in stone.

PLATE 10

ENIGMATIC URN

THIS singular draped stone urn found in the ancient St. Francisville Cemetery, has much of the suggestiveness of the revealing, yet featureless, heads placed on Chirico's painted figures of enigma. There is a hint here of a kind of inhuman personality. Below the urn, it will be noted, appear the poppies of sleep; still further down, Psyche, the butterfly, is carved; while the reverse side of the pedestal bears a sculptured image of a serpent swallowing its tail—the symbol of eternity. The character of this urn, and the particular use of the symbols here, is unique in Louisiana.

And here, in 1854, was buried Lewis Stirling, a planter who was not only the owner of Wakefield Plantation, but who, at his death, left the astounding proviso that the house be divided into three parts among his four heirs—and who must have been a classic scholar as well as a gentleman—a gentleman now sleeping forever under the aegis of the marble butterfly!

PLATE 11

DOORWAY TO FORGOTTEN YEARS

The Trépagnier House (About 1770)

THE great cavalcade of wealth and power in the lower Mississippi valley led, in time, to an architectural efflorescence unparalleled, both in extensiveness and originality of feeling, by anything occurring elsewhere in the United States of the 19th century. The beginning of this amazing architectural expression took source in such a house as we see here.

It is the raised cottage known as the Trépagnier House, built about 1770, and in it can be found the oldest known method of wall construction used in colonial times in Louisiana—clay packed between cypress studs, the clay being mixed with oyster shells and moss as a binder. The lower walls were, of course, entirely of plastered brick; while the upper colonettes were of carved cypress. The house is one of the few remaining from its period.

It was built by Jean Francois de Trépagnier, whose brother built Ormond (see Plates 12 and 13), and whose family was among the earliest in the colony. A member of the family left France for Canada in the seventeenth century; later descendants came to Louisiana and have remained here till this day. Jean Francois de Trépagnier met his death in 1811, at the hands of a band of rebellious slaves led by a servant who had become embittered by the master's failure to keep his promise of freeing him when he became of age. After this tragic event, the house was abandoned by the remainder of the family, and about it settled, as the years steadily deposited their webs of forgetfulness about the place, only a vague aura of sorrow. But amazingly, it has survived; although now in a state of advanced decrepitude. From this decay, the beautifully proportioned door and fan window emerge like an architectural vision—literally a door giving entrance to the shadows of other years; to an age forgotten.

PLATE 12

THE SHADOWS OF PEACE

Ormond Plantation (Before 1790)

THE spectre of tragedy, it seems, has forever darkened the history of Ormond, and the lives of its owners. It was built sometime before 1790 by Pierre de Trépagnier—brother of the unfortunate owner of the house shown in the preceding plate—who received the land as a reward by the Spanish Governor Bernardo de Galvez for his valorous activities against the English around Natchez. Pierre, who became, for a while, a very successful planter, was, too, involved in a tragic and mysterious end. In 1798, after a hasty whispered conversation with a stranger who refused to give his name to any save the master, Pierre went off in a carriage. The woods swallowed them. Pierre never returned. Nor was the mystery ever solved. After a year of agonized waiting, the disconsolate widow left the house forever; and the Butler family, famous in American Revolutionary history, as well as in the military history of Louisiana, bought it. Richard Butler, after the end of the War of 1812, settled here, and named the house after Ormond Castle in Ireland, the home of James Butler, Earl of Ormond. The Butlers grew in power and prestige, but in 1820 many of the leading members of the family were swept away by the yellow fever pestilence, and the McCutchons, who had married into the family, took over. It was they who demolished the two square *pigeonniers* to either side of the house, and replaced them with two two-storied wings. But this was done with such architectural ingenuity that the three buildings became an integral unit.

The McCutchons prospered. A merchant marine family, the house was filled with fine furniture and other objects brought by their ships from Europe. But in the 1870's they, too, had to abandon the house—beset by a host of economic reverses brought on by the Civil War. Ormond was overwhelmed by the black days of Reconstruction and passed through various, and less distinguished, hands. Among others, a man named LaPlace owned it, but one morning his body, riddled with bullets, was found hanging from a live oak. Again, no solution could be found.

Ormond softened and crumbled. In its later years, just before the last World War, it harbored a Negro family. Plate 12 shows it as it was then. Towards it stretch the shadows of peace. May they, after the tragic and turbulent years, rest forever there!

PLATE 13

THE RUINOUS COLUMNS

Ormond Plantation (before 1790)

ORMOND is among the outstanding examples of the early provincial architecture of Louisiana. It exhibits a number of indigenous features, coming, as it did, long before the grandiose houses showing classic influence. The central part of the house, which is the earlier portion, consists of four rooms to a floor, arranged in a square; and is constructed of a heavy cypress frame, filled in with mud and moss and bricks, and lathed and stuccoed over. The timbers are all mortised, tenoned, and pegged together. The wings, each totaling four rooms, are of solid brick, however; and there are covered galleries between them and the main house. The rounded columns of the lower main floor are of plastered brick, but the colonettes above are, as usual, of carved cypress wood. The roof, of shingles, had a lovely soft slope. So well were colors used in Ormond—lemon-yellow for the walls of the main house and the second floor of the wings (where it acquired a different nuance because of its more exposed weathering), pale green for the shutters and blinds, an incredibly soft white for the pillars and the first floor of the wings—that the house merged subtly and completely with its landscape. Clustered behind the building, in the time of the Butlers, were thirty slave cabins, a stable, a hospital, a meat storage house, and a jail.

Nowhere in this old house could one find a single completely vertical or horizontal line—everywhere there were exquisitely soft and crumbling edges, a wholly non-mechanical quality, as Plate 13 shows, due to the hand work everywhere.

Though in the last stages of impending collapse when this picture was made, its charm and innocence of feeling seemed, if anything, to have grown stronger with the years.

But although its doom seemed imminent, it has, within the last few years, been restored. It is due wholly to the efforts of Mr. and Mrs. Alfred W. Brown of New Orleans that this retrieving of the house from destruction has occurred.

PLATE 14

IN THE SHADOWS

Parlange Plantation (mid-eighteenth century)

NO MORE charming a house can be found, perhaps, among the early habitations of Louisiana than Parlange, whose history is enwrapped in legend and romance. The house was erected, some time in the 1750's apparently, by the Marquis Vincent de Ternant of Dansville-sur-Meuse, who obtained his land grant from the French crown. It was situated near "Fausse Riviere" (False River)—a cut-off arm of the Mississippi that had become a long and lovely lake without outlet.

The Marquis augmented his original wealth by the planting of indigo; and later, when insects threatened to make indigo planting impossible, he turned to sugar, becoming one of the earliest, and most successful, of the sugar planters. In 1757 he died; and his son Claude Vincent de Ternant went forward with the management of the plantation. Of Claude's first wife, Dorothée Le Gros, little is known; but his second, Virginie Trahan, was to become the animating force behind Parlange through much of the nineteenth century. Having borne her husband four children, Henri, Julie, Marius, and Marie Virginie—she proceeded to prove her distinction on the social plane by conquering the sophisticated and critical society of Paris during their frequent trips to the French capital. Her taste was proven by her choice of the magnificent furnishings which, each year, were sent back to the plantation from Europe. Henri, a child, went to his death by drowning in a small stream on the plantation. But it was she who, iron-willed, drove Julie to madness by her insistence on a marriage with a titled man Julie did not love. And it was she who so spoiled handsome young Marius that he became a wastrel, dying at twenty-five without issue. Yet it was she, too, who in the years succeeding Claude de Ternant's death in 1842, saved the plantation from destruction at the hands of Union troops by her tact and her artful offering of all the good food and wine they wanted. And Virginie, it is further related, not only hid her most valuable possessions from the troops, but also a great sum of money in an iron box—which afterwards mysteriously disappeared, and was never recovered.

Some years after the death of Claude de Ternant, Virginie, in Paris at the time, took as her second husband Colonel Charles Parlange of the French Army. By him she had one son, and it was this son who, with the help of Virginie, managed to save the plantation from utter ruin in the bitter years after the Civil War. Not only this, but he rose, after a difficult and lengthy struggle, to a justice of the Louisiana Supreme Court. Meanwhile, Virginie having died, Parlange lay abandoned for twenty years; till some time after the first World War, when Walter Charles Parlange, grandson of Virginie, returned with his young bride to the house— then the haunt only of owls and rodents. Called by some obscure voice from out of the past, they have together made Parlange again a living and beautiful thing.

PLATE 15

WHITE AGAINST GRAY

Parlange Plantation (mid-eighteenth century)

ARCHITECTURALLY, it is not easy to analyze the charm of Parlange. Possibly we cannot come closer to it than to say it rises from an utter simplicity, a simplicity so delicate, so wholly appropriate to the nature of its materials, that it becomes subtly beautiful. The house is surrounded by a magnificent array of oaks and cedars, attired in moss that darkens all the air. Against this accentuation of darks, the indescribably soft whites of the walls and columns seem all the more luminous. Plate 14—showing a side elevation of the house (the tree at the right is towards the front of the house) evidences this.

The bricks for the plastered columns of the first floor were handmade in triangular molds. All the fine woodwork detail—including the door and window frames—were hand-turned; the ceilings of the parlors made of cypress boards so dexterously fitted that they seem of plaster. Even the ceiling medallions are of carved wood, despite their deceptive appearance of plaster. In the lovely fan transoms delicate muntins have been developed from a flower theme. Many of the windows below, and even a few above, are iron-barred, giving mute testimony of the frontier origin of the house.

But not quite all is as it originally was with the house, however. The present open front stairs is probably of later date; since the true Louisiana Colonial houses had their exterior stairs beneath the galleries. And in the 1840's Virginie added extra rooms to the back of the house, making a double lower colonnade necessary in the rear.

Looking again at Plate 14 we are struck by the way the wide, open galleries, the exquisitely slim colonettes produce such a strong (and climatically functional) accentuation of horizontals that we are reminded, almost inevitably, of the use of deck-horizontals on certain houses by such modern architects as Frank Lloyd Wright and Le Corbusier. And then, it occurs to us, too, that Wright's Robie House in Chicago and Le Corbusier's Savoye House near Paris are not greatly dissimilar in basic plan from such a house as Parlange. . . .

Admirably situated some distance from the front of the house are two octagonal plastered brick *pigeonniers* (pigeon houses) with wooden finials. Their proportions, their whole design, are imbued with the feeling of northern France; since, at that time, Louisiana plantation buildings were still fairly close to the provincial architecture of the mother country. It is one of these we see in Plate 15, and to the foreground is a section of a decayed and fallen tree, like a weird dead monster. Around it moss has gathered—a ghostly conclave. It is extremely difficult to convey the true emotional quality of moss. Because of its amazing powers for the absorption of light, it usually appears as a vague dark blur in most photographs. But here its strange grayness, so dry and sharp, has sinister suggestions, the very textures imparting a feeling of suffocation. Having slain the great tree, it draws closer to this white survival from other years; like a grim rain of time.

PLATE 16

THE MIRROR OF LONG AGO

Parlange Plantation (mid-eighteenth century)

BETWEEN the chaste and colonial simplicity of the exterior of Parlange, and its sumptuous interior, there is a dramatic contrast. For the house was filled with treasures from the sophisticated nineteenth century artisans of Europe. Much of it remains, even today. Marvelously fine furniture: Louis XIV and Empire periods, inlaid tables, carved mahogany beds, Sèvres and Dresden vases, hand-painted china, brass cornices, figurines, paintings, whale-oil lamps, and mirrors, always mirrors, in all sizes and all shapes.

Over the fine mantel of the main salon there is a great mirror set about with an elaborate Louis XV filagree frame. Into its depths we peer, fascinated, and like an incredible and breathless vision from out of the past, a phantom floats upward, from the crowded and glittering rooms—the wraith of poor mad Julie, perhaps, who knew so little happiness in this house —or, at least, a *revenant* from the world within us, the world of the imagination, which is fed by our blood streams, and mysteriously allied with the past. And this apparition, hovering between the ornate candle brackets and the subdued scintillations of the chandelier, conveys to us mutely the very feeling of the magnificence of life in Louisiana's great plantation houses; particularly in those where the art of living drew discrimination and enrichment from its direct connection with the culture of France; conveys to us, too, the melancholy delight of the long ago and the far away. While below, the clock, shadowed by an enigmatic figure, secretively and untiringly adds more hours to the endless chain of hours which must have elapsed since this singularly lovely house first came into being.

PLATE 17

TRIUMPH OVER TIME

Voisin Plantation (about 1785)

FOR more than one hundred and twenty-five years the Voisin family has lived in the house seen in Plate 17. Its original round plastered columns have been replaced with later square brick piers; and the shingled roof with sheet metal. Aside from this, it has much of its original feeling, and is pure Louisiana Colonial; the plastered brick walls below; with spliced, mortised and interlocked timbers above, filled between with mud and moss, and lacking, characteristically, a central hall. One of the partly exposed clay-packed timbers can be glimpsed in the gallery wall to the left of the picture.

The plan of the main floor of the house is a simple one—three rooms wide, and one room deep. It is a plan found in most of the early Colonial houses, with but few exceptions—Parlange, and Ormond, are among these exceptions. The only stairs, an exterior one, rises from within the gallery space—another typical arrangement.

The survival of this house represents not only a triumph over time, but a triumph over the river, since it has had to be moved far back from its original site in order to be saved from the tremendous and stealthy convulsive movements of the Mississippi.

PLATE 18

FROM CHILDHOOD'S LOST WORLD

Voisin Plantation (about 1785)

AN OLD faded photograph of Miss Lydia Voison, present owner of Voisin Plantation, as a little girl of seven, furnished the starting point for this poetic interpretation. Behind her we see the house, strangely lost now, strangely swept by the conflagration of time, that burns clean our memories. But not wholly yet.

For we remember again, and with a pervasive nostalgia that recalls not individuals merely, the face with its beguiling and impish charm—the face of childhood, with its impossible, yet persuasive sweetness. We remember the sentient grace and suppleness, the amazing resilience, the infinite fluid potentialities—before they had frozen into commonplace and disquieting replicas of ourselves. And as we remember, some lost tragic portion of our beings finds re-creation—wandering somewhere vainly in closed, blind rooms of time.

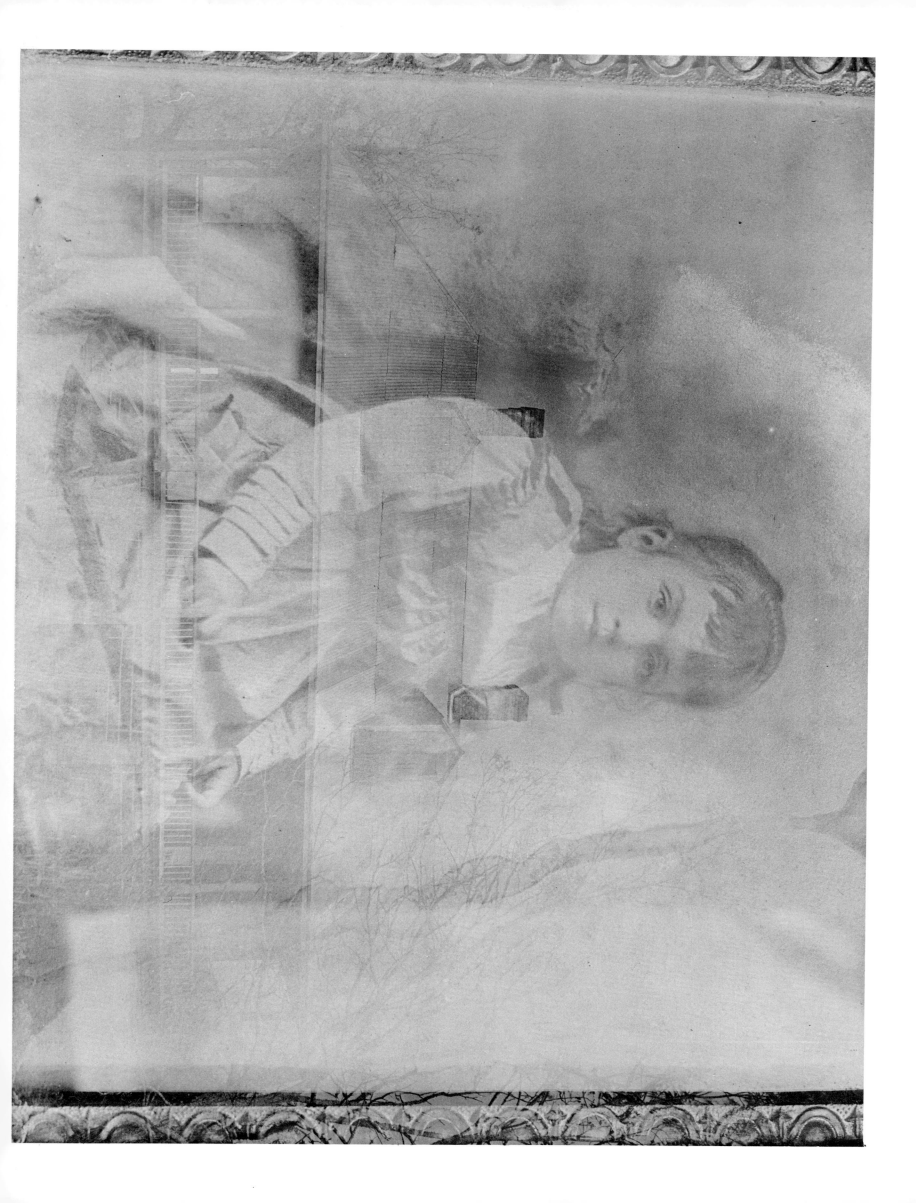

PLATE 19

IN SORROWFUL LIGHT (NO. 2)

Labatut House (About 1790)

SOMETIME in the last decade of the eighteenth century Don Evarist de Barra, a Spanish nobleman, had built for himself, by slave labor, the house now known as Labatut. A sister of de Barra later married a son of General Jean Baptiste Labatut, who had acquitted himself well in the defense of New Orleans under Andrew Jackson; and who had come to Louisiana in 1781. In time, the house passed into the hands of the Labatut family, whose descendants are still in possession of the house to this day.

But the years have not treated it gently. The grove of great oaks once fronting the house is now entirely gone, and the levee has moved almost upon the building. In melancholy light it looms, trembling upon the verge of destruction.

PLATE 20

THE LOST DOORS

Labatut House (About 1790)

LABATUT has been considered, rightly, by architects as a gem because of its fine detail. In addition, it is very important when regarded as a transition between the original Colonial style, and the composite or Louisiana Classic style of the grand houses which were to follow. For here are the plastered brick walls and pillars below, the wooden, above; but here, too, and among the first instances we know of, were the wide central hall, with the rooms arranged to either side; and delicate Georgian details in the transoms and sidelights— all of which were harbingers of the houses to come. The light and airy railing, too, is directly related in feeling to such later, and typical, railings as we find on Uncle Sam (Plates 69 and 70), and Oak Alley Plantations (Plates 50 and 51). The gallery to the rear of the house, where the stairs are located, is partially closed in by a room at each end; and looked down on what was, at one time, a flowered courtyard with a marble sundial.

No, the hours have not passed without their scars here; and we feel this intensely as we see, in the sadly revealing light, the delicate doors standing behind the simple picket fence, rough and green-gray with mould—doors lost, indeed, in time.

PLATE 21

THE GREAT GRAY CLOAK

Tomb of the Valcour Aime Family (St. James Cemetery)

WITHIN the engloomed tomb seen in Plate 21 lie some of the more prominent members of the Aime family. The greatest of these was Valcour Aime himself—who has been called, with little exaggeration, the Louis XIV of Louisiana. In the 1830's Valcour Aime practically rebuilt the old plantation structure left him by his father, and which dated back to the 1790's.

The new house became one of the most magnificent of all the Louisiana Classic houses, and was the heart of a 9,000 acre plantation. About its immediate environs there grew up an amazing kind of fantasy, now only a memory, and an almost unbelievable one. Facing it, at some distance, was a series of lagoons, over which were stone bridges with parapets; nearer by were gardens filled with wisteria, roses, jessamine, honeysuckle, clematis, lilies, and other blooms; in a series of conservatories were exotic plants from the Orient and Central America, including pineapples, mangoes, and coffee. At one point was an artifical hill with a grotto, crowned with a pagoda with tinkling bells; further, an artificial lake with a carefully constructed small fort whose cannon boomed welcome to the guests. In the gardens were peacocks and birds of all kinds; in the waters, fish and swans and pelicans; in a wooded area, rabbits, deer—and among all things—kangaroos! The house itself had its first floor made of black and white marble diamonds; its second floor of stone, its three great staircases of marble; secret stairways were built into the thick walls.

And the man who was the master of all this fantasy, Valcour Aime, was no secluded dreamer, but one of the most remarkable men in Louisiana history—scientist, planter, philosopher, and financier—whose income, at one time, was well over $100,000 yearly; who could serve a dinner ranging from fish to coffee, cigars, and wines—all produced from his plantation; who led the way in scientific experimentation with sugar cane culture; who operated a private steamboat from New Orleans for the use of his guests; who, despite his great wealth, had a highly developed sense of social responsibility; and who, despite all his achievements, his energy and his vision, could suddenly and completely collapse upon the unexpected death of his only son from yellow fever in 1854, writing this last entry in his diary: "Let he who wishes, continue; my time is done—he died on September 18. I kissed him at 5 o'clock—also on the following day. . . ." From this day, all scientific experimentation was stopped; his energy and his acumen seemed to desert him; he became a recluse, dying from pneumonia in 1867.

In the second decade of this century, this great house, from which all the magnificent furniture had been stolen, burned to the ground. . . . From its nearly concealed foundations now grows the conquering jungle, thick and well nigh impassable; in its lagoons, partially filled in, lies green-black loathsome water, like the dread water of nightmare; its bridges are gripped in the inhuman limbs of vine and root entities. Only the mosquito with its eerie whispering of yellow fever; the snake, with its cold slithering, and insects unnumbered and innominate, now keep vigil here. Only these, and the spectral sway of the moss. . . . Seen from a distance, the thick growth of jungle over the ruins, standing isolately in the comparatively cleared countryside, seems to harbor, even in the brightest day, a special and endemic darkness, a nameless night. . . .

And now, the Aime family sleep, with the great ghostly cloak of the moss above them, like the shadow of oblivion—the oblivion that has so completely overcast the works of Valcour Aime.

PLATE 22

UNDER THE OAKS (NO. 1)

Rienzi Plantation (close of the eighteenth century)

RIENZI is quite unlike its Louisiana neighbors of the same period in several respects. Perhaps this is because it was not built for one of the Creoles, but rather, we are told, for a man said to be the representative of Queen Maria Louisa, consort of Charles IV of Spain. Whether the Queen intended to use this place as a refuge because of the social unrest and military reverses Spain was encountering is not clear; but at any rate, in 1803, after Louisiana had passed from Spain to France, and then to the United States, Juan Ygnacio de Egana, the Queen's former representative, bought it, and lived here for nearly a half century. At some uncertain later date an Italian is said to have owned the plantation, and named it after Cola di Rienzi, the fourteenth century Italian patriot. Later, Judge Richard H. Allen took possession; and finally, the Levert family, who restored the house and still own it. It is usually included in the Spring Fiesta, and has been much admired.

The structure is of cypress, cedar and brick. Originally, the lower floor was entirely open and was used to stable horses; at some time previous to 1850 it was walled in and four more rooms thus added. The square brick piers and upper wooden columns are treated differently from the Louisiana Colonial houses; some feeling directly Spanish in character is indicated, too, by the elaborate interior woodwork, and the arrangement of the four upper rooms about a cross-shaped hall.

The house is noted for its double exterior stairs, gracefully curved for part of their ascent; for its huge main door; and for the gigantic live oaks, more than a century old, which set the building, from wherever one looks, in a series of living and dramatic frames.

PLATE 23

IN TRAGIC LIGHT

Zenon Trudeau House (early nineteenth century)

LITTLE seems obtainable on the history of this house; aside from the fact that it was once the home of Dr. Edward L. Trudeau, of Saranac Hospital. But like Rienzi—though not for the same reasons—it possesses features which set it apart from the Louisiana houses of its time.

For one thing—the brick columns below are missing. Instead, we have panelled wooden columns which run the full height of the two floors. It is possible, of course, that there were brick columns at one time, and that they were replaced for some reason—perhaps the bricks were crumbling. The walls, however, are the usual plastered brick, but on both floors. A charming and novel note is contributed by the cypress cornices of the house, which have been carved into a scalloped design, beautifully weathered.

As we proceed to the rear we find (referring to Plate 23) a still more unusual arrangement. Two octagonal *garçonnières* which, apparently, were originally distinct from the house, have been so treated as to give the effect of turrets. These are complete with doors giving access to the gallery, as well as with fireplaces and chimneys of their own. A single dormer on the rear of the low-hipped roof is almost hidden by the heavy entablature. There is something about this house which suggests, vaguely and delightfully, southern France; but this writer knows of no other quite like it in feeling elsewhere in Louisiana.

The house, unfortunately, is in extremely bad condition; and is not likely to last much longer. To the right of Plate 23 the old cistern can be discerned, in which the inhabitants still catch rain water for drinking purposes. The elephant ear plants nearby drink the sun eagerly; but the light caresses the old worn walls tenderly and tragically.

PLATE 24

THE MAW OF TIME

Versailles Plantation Ruins (1805 or earlier)

IN THE LATE afternoon light we discern the last remains of Versailles—the erstwhile magnificent plantation home of Pierre Denis de la Ronde III; a house once crowded with treasures from Europe, and now thought to be among the very earliest of all the great plantation houses of Louisiana. Its owner had distinguished himself at the Battle of New Orleans and was one of the wealthiest planters of his time. His niece was the Baroness de Pontalba, who built the famous apartment buildings facing Jackson Square in the heart of New Orleans. Like Valcour Aime his abilities and vision would have made him unique anywhere. Having accomplished more than enough to secure his place in Louisiana history, he became possessed by a great architectural dream.

He planned to establish a city in this vicinity, a city to be called Versailles, a city that would re-create some of the splendor of its namesake and would, in time, outgrow New Orleans. His plans came to naught. Events and conditions he could not overcome, thwarted him.

Meanwhile, the house was a tangible symbol of his vision. There were spacious galleries, fine colonnades, huge windows, moldings and ornamentation that represented the height in the European taste of his period. Indeed, judging from the sparse accounts we have, this house seems to have been (at least as far as its interior details were concerned) perhaps the most purely non-provincial French in character of any Louisiana plantation house known to us. The one possible exception to this might be the house of the Chevalier de Pradel, known as Mon Plaisir, and erected in 1754 on the west bank of the river opposite New Orleans, and long since destroyed. The beauty of Versailles, and the beauty, too, of de la Ronde's nine daughters—who were known as the Muses—and of his son, known as Apollo—made the house a social center.

With Pierre de la Ronde's death, the house was sold; and like an iridescent bubble, his plans collapsed. In 1876 the house—the American memento of the splendor of eighteenth century France—was destroyed by fire. Only the broken brick walls now remain. . . . They are surrounded, it is true, by an iron fence as a protection, but this is of no avail against the gigantic moss-hung hackberry trees interspersed among the ruins, whose roots, together with a host of vines, are systematically and slowly bringing about their total collapse.

Between the ruins and the river stretches an alley of tremendous live oaks, planted in 1762, and heavily draped with moss. It was in this giant natural avenue—now mistakenly known as the Packenham Oaks—that part of the bloody nocturnal encounter of December 23, 1814, which opened the Battle of New Orleans, was fought.

And the broken arch in the ruins—which we see in the opposite plate—with the light revealing dramatically and mercilessly the complete and sinister hollowness of its cavity, opens like the awful and empty maw of time directly towards that fane of the forest where men watered the roots of the oaks with their blood. . . .

PLATE 25

FAREWELL TO THE PAST (NO. 7)

The Chateau des Fleurs (1808)

ONCE in the open country, the Chateau des Fleurs became engulfed by the growth of New Orleans. It was built in 1808 by David Urquhart, grandfather of the later famed actress, Cora Urquhart.

The Chateau des Fleurs—so called because of its lovely gardens—followed only in part, the pattern of the true Louisiana Colonial houses. Actually, it represented a transition from the Colonial to the Classic houses. While the upper walls were wholly wood, the usual wooden colonettes of the Colonial period here were faithfully followed in form—but were executed in plastered brick—a step towards the great two-storied brick columns to come. As in practically all the early houses, the woodwork was mostly dovetailed and pegged together.

In 1833 it was purchased by Alexander de Lesseps, affluent planter and cousin of the famed Comte de Lesseps, builder of the Suez Canal. Shortly after the Civil War it became the property of James Maumas, who, in turn, passed it to his daughter Mrs. Anita Meraux. This led to its being sometimes called the Meraux House. In 1939 it was left only a shell by a devastating fire. The recent 1947 hurricane managed to smash a good part of the shell.

Plate 25 shows what little there was left of the house in 1940—including the well-preserved fountain, with its pineapple design, a later addition to the garden. And on the shattered gallery, beneath the blackened rafters, we see the figure whose veil becomes an integral part of her form, whose haunting quality crystallizes the nostalgia felt for all dead beauty, and for all lovely things forever beyond recall.

PLATE 26

MEMENTOES OF UNRETURNING TIME

The Chateau des Fleurs (1808)

IT IS possible to use a still-life arrangement, at times, to convey the intrinsic quality of a building; or the tragedy of a house.

Against one of the walls of the Chateau des Fleurs, whose cypress is charred to the sheen of black velvet, were placed two mementoes of the mystery of time—an old faded and encrusted photograph, and a battered Victorian statuette, holding an enigmatic mass over its head. The image in the cracked photograph has the quality of a phantom returned out of the dark mist of the years; and uncannily enough, its features resemble those of the statuette; although, rationally, they could not possibly be identical.

PLATE 27

THE SHUTTERED HOUSE

Oakley Plantation (1808-1810)

JAMES PIRRIE, a wealthy Scot, built this house sometime between 1808 and 1810, and to it he brought his bride, Lucy Alston Gray. The house, following no set style, consisted of a brick basement above which were two frame floors with galleries to the front and rear, most of which were permanently shuttered.

The house was then, and for many years thereafter, surrounded by a natural paradise—an amazing profusion of trees and vines and flowers: magnolias, holly, beeches, poplars, pines, iris, camellias, wild honeysuckle, wild jasmine; and seemed, in addition, to be almost the heart of a kingdom of birds. To this rich domain, in 1821, Mrs. Lucy Pirrie brought John James Audubon—not then known as the great naturalist he was afterwards to become—as tutor for her lovely daughter, Eliza. Audubon spent many happy and fruitful days here; but left, finally, nettled after a misunderstanding with Mrs. Pirrie. Some years later, Eliza, against her mother's wishes, eloped with Robert Hilliard Barrow. In their flight to Natchez they encountered a flooded stream. Romantically, Robert carried his young bride-to-be across in his arms. Six weeks later he was dead from pneumonia.

Oakley passed to the Matthews family, related by marriage to the Pirries through the Bowmans of Rosedown (see Plate 46); and was lived in till 1944 when Miss Lucy Matthews was forced to leave it because of ill health. It was left without a human occupant, but with all its treasures still within.

In 1945 thieves broke into the house, stealing from its walls several fine portraits by Armand and Sully; and at some indeterminate time, treasure hunters dug up the bricks of the kitchen floor. When seen in late 1946, it was entirely alone for the first time in over a century—amid woods grown dense and wild. Approaching the house, it exuded a sense of intense withdrawn-ness, of shrinking solitude; and we sensed too, how in this secluded and shuttered retreat its last occupants, the wraiths of another day, found a final refuge from a world grown too strange, too hard, and too disturbing. . . .

But though the history of Oakley seemed closed, and it appeared consigned forever to the dark and dusty embrace of the past—in August 1947 came remission. Through the untiring efforts of the Louisiana Society of the Daughters of the American Revolution, in which Mrs. J. L. Stirling of Woodhill Farm and Mrs. Marius Wilkerson of Baton Rouge played prominent parts—the state of Louisiana acquired Oakley from Miss Rosalie Matthews, a remaining member of the family, residing in Washington, D.C.

PLATE 28

THE LAST CAMELLIA

Oakley Plantation (1808-1810)

IN THE thick dark forest behind Oakley can be found an old well, a sunken greenhouse, and an abandoned carriage, left from better days. With it, in late 1946, the picture opposite was created—a visual poem to Oakley.

For the house then stood empty, its life drained, its woods no longer a paradise, but then strangely quiet, strangely ominous—while the last camellia, held by a weeping figure in a carriage from another time, fell from nerveless fingers.

PLATE 29

UNDER THE OAKS (NO. 3)

Live Oak Plantation (1808-16)

THIS house is not to be confused with the house, near Rosedale, called Live Oaks. The Feliciana Live Oak Plantation is an earlier house. It was built, according to some accounts, between 1808 and 1816, according to others, as early as 1790. It came within the sphere of Spanish influence extending south from Natchez, although this is not true of the majority of the old houses in the Feliciana country; and this influence shows, apparently, in the unusually heavy plastered brick columns of the ground floor. The exterior stair is hidden behind the shrubbery at the right of the picture. Within, there are some quite fine wooden details—particularly the door and window frames—although some additions and changes have been made, undoubtedly, to the house. Hand-wrought hardware is still existent, also. It is thought to have belonged, originally, to the Ratliff family, but is now owned by Mr. and Mrs. William LeSassier.

Surrounded by its shrubbery it has, in the late afternoon light, a gentle charm.

PLATE 30
TENDER SHADOWS
Waverly Plantation (1821)

PATRICK McDERMOTT, a miller, brought to the Felicianas by Baron de Carondelet, obtained the Spanish land grant to this plantation in 1804. His daughter, Emily, married a young physician, Dr. Henry Baines, who built this house in 1821, and named it after his home in England.

In a state where the Georgian style never attained a predominating role, the details of this house are among the finest Georgian in Louisiana. The style shows perfectly in the delicate details of the entrances—the fan transoms, sidelights, and pillars. The house is entirely of wood, and the quality of the hand-carved moldings and mantels within is outstanding. Unusual, too, for houses of the period are Waverly's built-in cupboards and clothes closets.

John James Audubon taught dancing here to augment his finances; and "Flying Charlie McDermott", a son of the miller, is said to have experimented with a "flying machine" here in the 1850's, but with rather doubtful results. He was granted a patent on the machine, ante-dating the Wright Brothers by almost seventy years. He spent several fortunes, and almost broke his neck, attempting to realize his dream of giving ". . . a flying chariot to every poor woman far better than Queen Victoria ever rode in." At the same time, he vented his feeling that it was ". . . mortifying that a stinking buzzard and a stupid goose should fly, and man, the lord of all earth, should be any longer confined to the land and water." None of "Flying Charlie's" models ever proved completely successful, however. The heirs of Dr. Baines occupied the house till a few years after the Civil War, then for over twenty-five years it lay abandoned and neglected.

In 1921 Mr. and Mrs. George M. Lester bought the place, and spent much time and expense restoring it. Its former beautiful gardens, too, are being restored; and Waverly is included among the houses on the Audubon Pilgrimage in St. Francisville each spring. As we see it now, the light bathes it as tenderly as, it would seem, its delicacy deserves.

PLATE 31

PIONEER FRAME

Austerlitz Plantation (1852)

THE Breaux family, one of whom was a Chief Justice of the Louisiana Supreme Court, built Austerlitz in 1852. It was named after Napoleon's great victory over the Austrians and Russians in 1805. It represents, probably, one of the last structures to be built in the Louisiana Colonial tradition; though, by this time, the large central hall had appeared, and the front gallery had been extended to the sides and back, so that the house actually represents a transitional type. Much of the original fine wrought iron hardware can be found inside the house.

In 1886 it was purchased by the Rougon family, who have completely restored it, including a fine garden to the front, where there are now beautiful azalea and camellia plantings. Colonel Henry A. Rougon and his sister are the present occupants.

As we see it here, from the side, it is set in a frame appropriate for its age and character—the great broken branches of a tree shattered by lightning—a frame which calls to mind the pioneer world.

PLATE 32

SINISTER SHADOWS

The Cottage (The Conrad Place) (1825)

THERE happens to be another house of the same name in West Feliciana Parish, belonging to the Butler family. The present house, however, was erected later, in 1825, by Colonel Abner Duncan, and presented to his daughter and her husband, Frederick Daniel Conrad, as a wedding gift. No explanation has ever been advanced as to how so large a house ever received a name so indicative of modest size. It is one of the earliest still existing examples of the really great houses to show a definite classic influence—the Greek Revival, of course, being fused with some of the more local characteristics in such a way as to acquire, as has been pointed out in the Prologue, an indigenous quality.

The lower walls, which are two feet thick, support wooden walls above—an indication that this house was a step in the progression towards houses like Oak Alley. Most of the huge rooms, twenty-two in number, open on to deep galleries, which are probably the widest in the state—this arrangement permitting constant access to the river breezes. The plantation possessed both a sugar house and a cotton gin.

Jefferson Davis, Henry Clay, Judah P. Benjamin, President Zachary Taylor, General Lafayette were among the noted people who knew the hospitality of The Cottage. The landed property alone of the Conrad family, who were distantly related to George and Martha Washington, amounted to several millions of dollars. This did not include their jewelry, nor the sumptuous carriages and fine horses, nor the magnificent mahogany and rosewood furniture, most of which was seized by the Union troops. During the conflict the place was used as a yellow fever hospital by the Federals; and this fact saved it from being stripped by vandals during the many years it lay empty after hostilities ceased, since prospective looters were afraid of contracting the disease.

Mrs. J. J. Bailey, a descendant of the Conrads, and her brother have managed to pull the plantation back from ruin within recent years.

As we see it now, in the late lonely light, the darkness grown animate in the moving moss shadows, sweeps in on the house, swallowing the gallery to the right. And the pillars, glimmering with a brightness that seems waxing now because of the moving obscurity, appear to acquire a life of their own. Yes, they can resist still the shadows of decay; the night of ruin.

PLATE 33

THE SPECTRAL FANS

The Cottage (The Conrad Place) (1825)

THE Cottage, like most of the old plantation houses, has had a number of ghost stories associated with it, though in this case they seem to be particularly definite. Many an evening, it is said, finds strange music issuing from the upper gallery—some of the slaves it seems, who once gave impromptu musicales for the guests of the Conrads on these same wide galleries, have returned, singing and playing the songs of the fields. But a certain "Mr. Holt" forms the center of an even more persistent story. Originally, Mr. Holt was a secretary to Frederick Conrad. After their imprisonment together by the Union troops, and the death of Conrad subsequent to the War, Mr. Holt returned to the house. Perhaps because of the effects of his imprisonment, perhaps because of other reasons, he developed a peculiar fear of being totally impoverished. He saved scraps of everything, even had trunks of stale biscuits, and grew addicted to wandering around the rooms at night. Nor did this habit, seemingly, stop with his death, for he has been seen by a number of people it is said.

Perhaps, too, Mr. Holt saved substitutes for the fans so necessary in the Louisiana summers; and which were often made of the dried leaves we will presently mention. But even if he did not, and even if there are no ghosts of human beings to stalk these rooms at all, the spectral things we see in the opposing picture could easily be, perhaps, the wraiths of splendor, the phantoms of elegance. And these phantoms are made, not of the glittering fans that must once have graced the drawing rooms of this house (since these are forever gone) but, as seems more befitting, of the palmetto fronds which are so important an element in the special landscape of Louisiana, and which, dried and sown, formed the most common type of fan in this state in the nineteenth century.

PLATE 34

THE INCREDIBLE AVENUE

Pine Alley Plantation (1829?)

CHARLES J. DURANDE has become a mythical figure, even to his descendants. In a state which has been particularly fruitful in the strange and the fantastic — both in persons and in things—his is a niche by no means an inferior one. Possessed of enormous wealth, an enormous flair for life, and an equally expansive imagination, his deeds seem like the sheerest fiction. Yet they partake so integrally of the extravagant nature of plantation culture, that they cannot be dismissed as mere fables.

Sometime before 1820 Durande came to the country around St. Martinville. Just why he left France no one seems to know. Already possessed of huge wealth, he became the owner of thousands of acres, and shortly pyramided his wealth with sugar. The date of the establishment of his great house, again, seems uncertain; but the oak and pine alley leading to it is said to have been planted in 1829 by slaves. But, unlike anything in Louisiana it led a full three miles from Bayou Teche to the house! Among other things, his set of regal carriages, including even the harness, were ornamented with gold, and must have made a spectacle indeed when the family went driving. Each morning, too, slaves woke them with sprays of perfume, and the family learned to delight in bathing in water strewn with perfumed crystals—an unheard of refinement at that time.

By his first wife Durande had twelve children. When she died he was inconsolable, visiting her grave each day. Extreme in his grief as in all else, he had an iron statue of himself placed, kneeling, before her tomb; swearing never to marry again. Yet within a year Durande was wedded once more—untroubled by the bourgeois necessity of being consistent. By this second wife, too, his children numbered twelve. This, he considered, was the only fair thing for a man of honor to do!

But it was in 1850, on the occasion of the simultaneous wedding of two of his daughters, that Durande's imagination soared to really superb heights. For this event he had made special preparations. Large spiders—brought from China, according to some accounts—had been set free in the oak alley several days in advance. Great webs had been spun. And on the morning of the wedding the slaves were given bellows and gold and silver dust. With these the webs were coated. Beneath this utterly fantastic canopy, aerial and metallic, that billowed in the moving air, that quivered and glinted in the torch light when the sun descended—and over carpets spread between the trees—the couples were led. Lasting till nightfall, the wedding festivities included food and wine for two thousand guests. Durande, indeed, knew how to enjoy wealth!

But like a blight, the Civil War came, and in it, Durande lost everything. His slaves disappeared, his mansion was stripped, his crops ruined. He died shortly after the war's end. Eventually, the family scattered, and the house was left to the elements. Some years ago it was completely demolished. The last traces of Durande himself—several fine portraits by an unknown painter—were, with tragic irony, lost in the flood of 1927.

The alley remains; though now no more than a third of its former length. Unlike the great avenues at Oak Alley and Rosedown, which are far wider, Pine Alley, due to its comparative narrowness and enormous height, re-creates the true effect of a cathedral nave. And as we proceed down this mile-long and magnificent arcade, it comes like a shock to find only emptiness at the end. It is, we realize suddenly, like the life of Charles Durande himself. . . .

PLATE 35

ANCIENT DRAPES

Evergreen Plantation (1850?)

THE outlines of the history of Evergreen Plantation are, it must be acknowledged, hazy and conjectural in the extreme. The few available accounts seem not too accurate, and original source material appears either non-existent or inaccessible.

The available evidence indicates that the Brou family—who were from France; and the Becnel family—from England—were undoubtedly implicated in the development of the plantation. The date of the present main house is uncertain and the architect, if any, unknown. That all of the many buildings still left on the plantation are not of the same date seems fairly certain. Madame Pierre Becnel II made claim to the property in 1812, because of prior occupancy; and it may quite possibly be that an earlier, Colonial house stood on the spot now occupied by the main house. In any event, a Pierre Becnel married a Desirée Brou in 1830, and the plantation seems to have remained in the hands of the two families till the early 1890's, when the property was taken over by the Songy Brothers, and managed as a sugar plantation. Following this, the Marine Bank became the owner of the plantation, and then the Canal Bank. During this period the house lay neglected, and abandoned to the elements. In 1946 Mrs. Matilda Gray bought the entire property, and with Richard Koch as architect, has embarked on an ambitious and extensive program of restoration.

Along the borders of the property ran great lines of trees—three on the upstream side, and three on the downstream. The lines consisted of huge live oaks, somewhat smaller magnolias, and dwarf cedars—arranged in a scale of descending size—and this arrangement was repeated on the opposite side of the estate; each of the two outermost lines forming great alleys that extended all the way from the levee, past the main house, and then back to the cane fields. At the extreme ends of these alleys were the slave cabins, arranged on both sides of each alley—one group of these still exists. In the great cleared space before the main house there was, originally, a formal garden—such as can be found before the manoirs of France and the villas of Italy—its paths bordered with shells and rigidly patterned, its plots blazing with massed flowers. Behind the house was a wide lawn, bordered by accessory structures (see Plate 36), and some distance further, the kitchen garden and orchards. Then came the cane fields and sugar mill. Altogther, a typical and beautifully integrated arrangement.

Today, as we approach the house, we find that its beauty has never been completely extinguished, even during its darkest days; that, on the contrary, it has mellowed with time; and that there hovers about it an air of expectancy—as though it knows that a new day, and a new life, has come. And the gray and ancient drapes of the moss part, as though with reluctance, as though they were curtains opening on a new act in the life of the house—an act in which Evergreen will find a second, and happier, existence; will be more lovely, more gracious, more secure, than ever. . . .

PLATE 36

CLASSIC PRIVY

Evergreen Plantation (1850?)

THE main structure at Evergreen combines some of the features of the not purely Louisiana houses (such as those around St. Francisville), i.e. the use of pediments, and the roof deck with balustrades (this latter has been temporarily removed, but will be replaced—see Plate 35) with those more characteristic of the true Louisiana Classic style—the hipped roof, the one-room-deep plan, the wide galleries. Only here the encompassing of the galleries has been broken, possibly at a later date, by two small wing rooms, above and below, added to the original three-room-wide arrangement. The fact that a portion of the brick rear wall of one of the wing rooms has partly collapsed at one of the corners of the house (it was replaced, later, by wood) would suggest that structural changes, somewhat inferior in skill, did indeed take place later in the house Most unusually, a pedimented portico appears, very well proportioned, whose function was to receive the two fine free standing staircases that curved through the air to the second floor. One of these staircases disappeared many years ago. The other, showing masterly workmanship, has been temporarily removed so that it can be repaired and more exactly copied for the restoration of its twin. The rear stair comes up under the gallery; and originally, this may have been true, too, of the front stair, with the pedimented portico being added subsequently to receive the curved exterior stairs.

Within, there are a number of fine gray marble mantels; the trim exhibiting careful execution; window frames in which an acorn motif is carved in the wood.

Immediately flanking the house are two *pigeonniers*, one of which can be seen to the left of Plate 35. Somewhat to the right and left there are the *garçonniéres*; and then, walking away from the rear of the main house, we encounter two other buildings—one of these, the kitchen; the other, the office—with brick between posts construction. Internal structural evidence in these buildings—and in another building some distance upstream—now known as the "overseer's house"—strongly suggests that they antedate the main building. Possibly, the family originally lived in the "overseer's house" and then, as their wealth grew, had the big house built. Or if an older building existed on the present site of the main house, it may be that they lived in the "overseer's house" only while the new main building was being erected.

Be this as it may, as we wander further beyond the rear of the main house, we find that the former lawn has now become a lovely garden with small stone figures added to its corners; and at the furthermost corners of this space were the sites of two more buildings—carriage houses, it is thought. Midway between these was a little double privy, of plastered brick, executed in Greek Revival design—and now unique in Louisiana. No existing small building tells us so much, perhaps, nor so gracefully, of the height achieved in the art of living by Louisiana plantation culture, than this exquisite little privy; so delicately set off by the lustrous and lovely grays of the moss, and the dark figure of the cherub with his sheaf of wheat—the whole ensemble fascinating not only to the graphic sense of the photographer, but to the appreciation for beauty of anyone who beholds it. Now that Uncle Sam Plantation has been destroyed (see Plate 69) Evergreen has become the most complete plantation group still existent in Louisiana.

PLATE 37

THE ENSHADOWED PILLARS (No. 4)

Chrétien Point Plantation (1831-1835)

NO existing house, possibly, in Louisiana preserves more of its original flavor, and of the special character of plantation life than does Chrétien Point. It does this, perhaps, because it has been less tampered with; and because, too, ruin has not progressed nearly as far as with most of the unrestored houses.

Purchasing from Pierre Déclouet, around 1800, a tract of land granted by the Spaniards in 1776, Hypolyte Chrétien, another arrival from France, began to raise cotton. Also, he became an extremely good friend of Jean and Pierre Lafitte, the pirates and smugglers whose contraband goods were well received by even the best merchants of that time. In time his son, Hypolyte II, married the headstrong and dashing Félicité Neda, the daughter of a neighboring Spanish land-owner. Félicité had quite a reputation, which she later greatly enhanced, for unconventionality. Despite their many quarrels the newly married couple did achieve one thing in common—the fine house we now see in Plate 37. Shortly after its completion Hypolyte II was dead from yellow fever; and Félicité, with complete assurance, assumed management of the plantation, which now included as many as five hundred slaves. Never lady-like by the standards of the day, Félicité proved a capable manager; not only this, she became fond of cards, and through her proverbial luck, further extended her land holdings; also, even more shocking, she smoked. She had opportunity to prove her physical courage, too, for one night she shot off the head of a marauder who attempted robbery. But even her strength and energy had to end, and Hypolyte III, her only surviving son, ill and crippled, alone had to go on. He managed, though not as well as his mother; but it was he who saved the house when Union troops approached in 1863. Rising from his sick bed, he tottered to the upper railing, and with shaking and uncertain hands, made the Masonic sign. The Union commander, as it happened, was a Mason too, and the house was saved, though most of the accessory buildings were destroyed. By his wife, Celestine Can-trelle, he had had an only son, Jules. Sensitive and impractical, loving books and music and good talk, Jules was left to carry on in the grim years after the War. His magnificent library, mostly from France—Chateaubriand, Voltaire, Rousseau, Hugo—interested him more, however. He had to borrow; then when he did finally try to get the plantation in hand, by substituting rice for the now unprofitable cotton, it was too late. Jules was now heavily in debt, and the plantation mortgaged to the hilt. And he was simply untrained for any ordinary type of work. He became a peddler of kitchen utensils, going from door to door with his charming manners, his phrases of exquisite French.

Somehow, and by means at once amazing and tenacious, the Chrétien family held on. And today, Mrs. C. A. Gardiner, one of the remaining descendants, owns the house which, more than any other, is steeped in the authentic aura of Louisiana's lost plantation culture.

PLATE 38

UNDER TIME'S ONSLAUGHTS

Chrétien Point Plantation (1831-1835)

IN the Prologue it has been said that in the grand Louisiana Classic style — the style that
followed the Colonial period—the outstanding thing to be remembered was that it incorporated Classic Revival and Georgian influences into an ensemble so organized that it was
given an indigenous character. Chrétien Point is an excellent example of this statement. In
houses such as this the classic influence first definitely established itself. But it is easy to see
how the classic coldness of Greek Revival has been given an entirely different character here—
how much variance in feeling there is, for example, in the great columns alone because of their
being executed in plastered brick instead of the usual stone. Or how the entablature has acquired
a new quality, and a fresh treatment, because cypress wood was the material used. (Incidentally,
even the gutters of Chrétien Point still exist in their original material—cypress wood—though
this is not commonly mentioned.) We can see, too, how the subordinate Georgian influence
showing in the deep arched windows and doors has assumed an endemic flavor because of the
special integration which has been achieved.

Chrétien Point took four years to build. There is still in existence a contract between Hypolyte II and Samuel Young and Jonathan Harris as carpenter and bricklayer and "undertakers
of building". Such an arrangement as this document, with its vague specifications, indicates
was a not unusual one, and an important conclusion can be drawn from it. In many of the great
houses in the first half of the century, at least, the architect was actually no one person, but was
represented by a common and cooperative working arrangement between the owner and the
master artisans—a communal concept, related to the nature of the times, and the materials, was
in their minds, and towards this all labored. It was the frequent absence of a formal architect
(who, trained elsewhere, would have been less sensitive to local influence), and the resultant
cooperation between the owner-designer and the craftsmen which was, undoubtedly, one of the
most important factors in the appearance of so many houses in Louisiana with such strongly
indigenous quality.

The walls of the house were 18″ thick; its plan, three rooms across, and one and a half deep;
the roof is hipped and (originally) shingled; and the great Tuscan columns, as in most cases at
the beginning of the absorption of classic influence, form a single colonnade along the façade
of the house.

If the communal builders of this period knew how to integrate materials, they knew, too,
how to integrate colors. Within, in a secluded and smaller room can be found plastered walls
whose exquisite greenish-yellow recalls nothing so much as the gown of the woman in Picasso's
tender and beautiful "The Lovers". Another room has a blue reminiscent of the delicate and
sensitive blue in the same painting—not at all like the effeminate pastel blues to which we have
grown so accustomed by purveyors of paint to housewives.

Outside, the house blends beautifully into its setting. Some of the gray of the moss has seeped
into the white of the woodwork and great pillars; the greenish blinds are, also, subtly blue, as
though from the sky; while the incredibly soft red in the exposed brick of the walls forms an
effective transition between the two. And the windows, catching reflections from the trees and
moss, darkly gleam, as though with profound and mournful thoughts of the long ago.

PLATE 39

A PLASTER MASTERPIECE

Chrétien Point Plantation (1831-1835)

THE present occupants of Chrétien Point, who are only tenants, inhabit but a few of the rooms downstairs. Upstairs, we find magnificent mantels left of verde antique marble with black onyx caps and shelves.

The original fine furniture has been removed long since. With the tragic and terrible irony which seems to dog so many of the houses and their owners, these possessions had been moved to the small town of Jennings, where a modest hotel had been started by one of the last of the Chrétiens in the attempt to retrieve the family fortunes; and everything lost in a disastrous fire.

Equally excellent as the general treatment of the house is its superb plaster work. And, as we look up to the lovely medallion on the ceiling of the upper salon we see how its delicate acanthus leaves, one by one, have been dropping into the whirlpool of time.

PLATE 40

SMOKE OF DESTRUCTION

Linwood Plantation (1835?)

ON land acquired by Philip Minor, one of whose ancestors had been Stephen Minor, governor of Natchez under the Spanish, Linwood was built at some uncertain date, probably in the 1830's, but perhaps as late as the 1840's, since it is attributed to the great architect James Gallier, Sr. Gallier erected another huge house, Ashland, in the vicinity in 1841.

Its floor plan made Linwood unique among the houses of Louisiana. Whenever wings were used on the other Louisiana houses of the period—which was not often—they were made definitely subordinate; Woodlawn (Plates 93 and 94) and Madewood (Plates 66 to 68) are examples of this. Here, however, the enormous two-storied and colonnaded wings were to extend outwards a great distance, at direct right angles to the main axis of the house. The Roman Doric columns of the main part of the structure, six in number, supported a great fan-windowed pediment. At the opposite end of the building was a portico with two columns supporting a smaller pediment. Galleries ran along one side of the wings. In the opposing plate, one of the wings is seen (to the left) only in small part, while the other wing appears missing. What happened was this: during the Civil War Union troops burnt one wing completely (the rest of the house was saved by slaves), and this wing was later replaced by a small temple-like structure. Below, the usual central hall in the main building was apparently converted in later years to an improvised porte-cochère, by tearing out the door frames and floors. This was while this part of the structure was being used to stable farm animals. Originally, the halls had an unusual feature—they were covered by hand-painted wallpaper panels representing, according to a contemporary visitor in 1849, fantastic jungle scenes, savages, lairs of ferocious beasts, snakes, peacocks, and parrots.

Judging from the plan above, it would seem Gallier had in mind the great Palladian villas of the Brenta, in Italy. If so, once more Louisiana materials superimposed their own feeling on the derived architectural influences. But, in any event, this beautiful building seems to be one of the earliest and greatest of Gallier's triumphs in the domestic architecture of the plantations.

When Union troops sacked the house, they removed, or put to the torch all of its furniture and paintings. The marble mantels and silver-plated door knobs disappeared, as well. Towards 1900 the house was abandoned by the last of the Minors. In 1939 the house was demolished by the present owners of the plantation because of the excessive cost of restoration; and to obtain the bricks in it. As we see it, Plate 40, it was in the process of destruction; its roof and pediments had already been ripped off. Toward the left, with dreadful finality, clouds are rising, like the smoke of destruction.

PLATE 41

THE LUMINOUS COLUMNS (NO. 1)

The Hermitage (1812-1814, and remodeled about 1849)

IN 1812, Michel Doradou Bringier — son of one of the great early Louisiana plantation families — took to wife lovely Aglaé Du Bourg, who was then fourteen years old. The War of 1812 was drawing towards the Battle of New Orleans, and soon the young Michel found himself an aide to Andrew Jackson, of whom he became an ardent admirer Tendering the General a victory entertainment at his new house, which had just been finished, Michel decided to call it The Hermitage—after the General's Tennessee home. It was a name most uncommon for a Creole house, but they took care of that shortly; it became l'Hermitage.

Michel died in 1847, but Aglaé, undaunted and calm, as in all things, went on with the affairs of the plantation. During the Civil War, the house was saved, though damaged somewhat from a cannon ball which smashed through one of the windows. After the termination of the war, Louis Amédée Bringier, a son of Michel, who had become a Colonel in the Confederate army, came back to attempt a fresh start. Against all odds he succeeded, and the plantation, with the help of some of the slaves who returned as freed men, became again a great sugar producer. It was in these years that a huge brick sugar house was erected, above which was placed on a shaft, a large gold-leaf covered globe, as a symbol of prosperity. Following all this, Colonel Bringier sold the property to Duncan Kenner, from whom it passed, in the late 1880's to the Maginnis family, and then, through various hands, to Wilmon Duplessis. In 1945 Mrs. Rene La Salle and her son, Arthur, became the owners, their intent being, in time, to restore the house completely in conformance with its original character—even to a now missing two-storied structure, added behind the main house some time in the 1820's, and which contained a magnificent ballroom above, with black marble mantelpieces. This structure was destroyed in the 1930's.

Irrefutable evidence of The Hermitage's early origin can be found in its very thick walls, some of which are brick between posts. In the great attic all the heavy beams are held together with huge pegs. Evidently, too, the house has undergone some remodeling. This seems to have happened about 1849, and, possibly, at the masterly hands of James Gallier, Sr. In conformance with its colonial origin, it appears that it originally had an encircling gallery with the typical brick columns and wooden colonettes—this is certainly true of the ballroom structure, as shown by an old photograph. The columns and colonettes of the main house only were replaced by great Tuscan pillars, the stairs probably re-located, and the deep galleries set back to barely touch the pillars, thus allowing the latter to obtain their maximum effect.

So excellent is the proportioning of this house—the height and weight of the pillars, for instance, compared with the dimensions of the doors and windows, and the size of the cornices—that probably not a single measurement could be changed without impairing the beautiful integration which has been achieved. And withal, there is about this house a purity of line and mass that allies itself with the objectives of the best modern architecture. As we see it now in Plate 41, the softly textured, and exquisitely rounded pillars are set off by the dark diagonal of the great live oak, and the variant tones of the old French picket fence. The pillars of this house are rightly considered among the finest in Louisiana. And we see, too, how the beautiful and luminous quadrangle stands forth in the light, while it encloses a house resting—with a sense of infinite peace—in the shadow.

PLATE 42

THE LUMINOUS COLUMNS (NO. 2)

Greenwood Plantation (1830-1835)

WILLIAM RUFFIN BARROW, descendant of an English family who first settled in the Carolinas, and then came to the beautiful Feliciana country around 1803, built Greenwood in the period 1830-35. It was set on a tract of 12,000 acres, on land granted by the Spanish to Oliver Pollock in the eighteenth century. Pollock, with the cooperation of Governor Galvez of Louisiana, had helped the American colonies to the extent of $300,000 during the Revolution; and then had sold the land to the Barrows while in debt.

The Barrows prospered and became one of the most influential families in this section; building, also, a number of other houses. But seeing the indications of impending conflict, the house was sold in the 1860's to the Reed family. Federal troops destroyed all of the numerous out buildings during the war, but the house itself was saved as a hospital. In 1906, the Reeds, no longer able to hold the house, sold it to Mr. and Mrs. Frank S. Percy, who undertook the numerous necessary restorations.

A great central hall 70 feet long, runs through the house, dividing the usual four rooms. From this hall, a mahogany staircase rises to a second floor with the same plan. There are marble mantels, Irish and Belgian lace curtains, much fine silver, including a venison dish from England. The furniture of the dining room is hand-carved English oak; that of the parlor, rosewood Louis XV covered with Aubusson tapestry. The panelled cypress doors bear door knobs and hinges of silver.

In Plate 42 we look diagonally toward the house; its main entrance is on the side to the right of the picture.

PLATE 43

MOSS FINGERS

Greenwood Plantation (1830-1835)

ARCHITECTURALLY, Greenwood differs in a number of important respects from those houses further south which we may correctly regard as the arch-types or best exemplifications of the feeling and developments most indigenous to Louisiana. For one thing, the usual second floor gallery is completely missing. At once, this demonstrates the presence of some Eastern seaboard influence at Greenwood—an influence also present later, though in more temperate a form, at The Houmas House (Plate 56). Then, too, the columns spring from a raised porch which is, actually, almost the height of a man, instead of flush with the earth as in the pure Louisiana Classic houses. Also, the entablature of the twenty-eight Doric pillars displays mutules, triglyphs, and guttae—all of which are completely absent, usually, from the structures more peculiar to Louisiana. Finally, instead of finding brick walls here, we find plaster over laths. However, the columns are of the customary plastered brick, and entirely encircle the 100-foot-square building.

Greenwood was four years in building, and probably another year was needed for all the accessory structures. These, originally, numbered some forty, we are told: stables, kitchens, coach houses, a smoke house, a hospital, a church, sugar houses, and cotton gins—also there were about a hundred brick slave cabins. It was a complete community—even to the large sunken cisterns, made of bricks; an artificial lake, a race track, and a deer park. It represented an integration completely non-urban; the height of an agricultural civilization.

As we walk slowly around Greenwood, with its imposing and lofty columns we come, in sunset's lingering and nostalgic light, to the rear of the house. A great dead tree rises; from it weird gray shapes seem to throng towards the lonely and supernal beauty of the pillars, given life by the light. And the great hand of the tree, clothed in moss—the robe of things dead—reaches its gaunt dripping fingers, in the failing light, towards the living and lustrous thing which is Greenwood.

PLATE 44
THE NEW AND THE OLD
Greenwood Plantation (1850-1855)

ONCE more we see Greenwood. But this time we are looking into the hub cap of a modern automobile—as though it were a magic opening in space—and we see a reflection of the house; providing a dramatic contrast between the new and the old. The old, with its beauty based on brick and wood; the new, with its basis on metal. The insignia on the hub cap spins up from the earth; the cloud rushes over the house. The black reflection of the photographer's hand and camera help the illusion of enormous depth.

PLATE 45

THE BASHFUL DISCUS THROWER

Oak Lawn Plantation (1827, restored in 1926)

THE original house of this name was built as early as 1827 by Judge Alexander Porter, famous Louisiana jurist. Among Judge Porter's friends was Henry Clay, who was often entertained here; and there can still be seen in the remodelled house the bath made from a single block of marble, which Clay is said to have used.

Colonel Robert E. Rivers, owner of the St. Louis Hotel in New Orleans, became its next owner shortly after the Civil War. But by the early years of this century it had gone into complete neglect, and was occupied by Negro squatters. Dr. Herman de Bachellé Seebold, who visited the house in 1925, comments extensively on it in his "Old Louisiana Plantation Homes and Family Trees", remarking on its huge size, its excellent detail, and the remains of the once lovely gardens of crepe myrtle, mimosa, oleanders, sweet olive, and other trees and shrubs.

It was a pedimented house, with colonnaded porticos to front and rear; and with a great central hall and fine spiral staircase of mahogany. The ballroom, unusually enough, was in the huge attic which had been plastered—its dimensions were 60 feet by 160 feet. In 1926 Captain Clyde Barbour began restoring it; but while this work was going on, a fire occurred which destroyed all of the house but its 14″ thick brick walls and columns. Within a short while, however, the house was completely rebuilt—following old photographs. But its character suffered transformation. Now there are marble floors—much of it said to be from the main hall of the famed old St. Louis Hotel—instead of the original cypress; and an iron staircase substituted for that of mahogany. Intimate knowledge of the house as it was, and as it is now, would be of great value in gauging just how much the special character found in the pure Louisiana Classic plantation style was dependent on local materials used.

The adjoining picture gives us only a glimpse of the present-day gardens at Oak Lawn Manor as it is now called. Louisiana sun and dampness have cracked off the arm of this fine marble statue, set in the gardens, and said to have been brought from Italy. Across its chest the rain has made a beautiful mottled pattern. Meanwhile, the vine—a vegetable Mrs. Grundy—cunningly censors its mid-section.

PLATE 46

MAGNIFICENT AVENUE

Rosedown Plantation (1835)

PERHAPS nothing prepares us so well for revelation as the grand alley leading to Rosedown—its arcade seeming to stretch without end—the golden glow sifting through the leafy vaults filling the air with a sense of infinite distance. The house seems lost in space, but by slow degrees it comes mysteriously closer. So clothed it is, however, in veil after veil of shrubbery, in cascades of leaves, that it never seems fully to reveal itself.

Enhancing the beauty of the avenue is an element setting it apart from all other plantation alleys now existing. Behind each line of oaks is a row of Carrara marble figures on brick pedestals—all gods and goddesses from Greek and Roman mythology. The great trees, not cleaned of moss, preserve all their sense of immemorial mystery; and a silence pervades in which it seems that nothing less soft than recollections should tread.

Daniel Turnbull, an Englishman, had this house built in 1835 for his young bride of eighteen whose family was the Barrows, mentioned in connection with Greenwood Plantation (Plate 42). She named it Rosedown from a romantic play seen in New York while they were on their way back from a tour of Europe. Later, they were to make more trips, and each time treasures were sent back to fill the house. Later, too, they were to have a daughter, Sarah, and Sarah became one of the most famed of the Feliciana beauties of her day. In time, Sarah, having refused innumerable offers, married James Pirrie Bowman, son of another great beauty, Eliza Pirrie (see Plate 27). By him she had two sons, and eight daughters. James Bowman, considered one of the most polished gentlemen of his time, had beautiful manners, but not enough business sense, it seemed. Following the Civil War, the property went into debt. Not only was the value of cotton declining, but it was not readily recognized that too much cotton had been drawn from the soil; that new agricultural knowledge was needed. Life was so pleasant; there were so many beautiful things to see and do; so many social affairs where the girls could display their charm, that hardly any heed was given to the spectre of poverty.

But when the spectre became reality, the Bowman sisters proved their mettle. With most of the servants gone, the girls did some of the manual work. Finally, after a long struggle against adversity, and with but three of the Misses Bowman left—the tense battle was won and the house rescued from mortgages. Today, the three old sisters—now like shells eaten hollow by memory—have still one more abiding memory—the memory of a nearly impossible triumph.

PLATE 47

IN THE SHADOW OF THE URN

Rosedown Plantation (1835)

IN still more pronounced a fashion than Greenwood even (Plate 42), the special feeling of the pure Louisiana Classic style seems to have been subordinated at Rosedown. Indeed, the house smacks strongly of a Virginia manor house. The two-story central structure is built entirely of cedar and cypress; it has a gabled roof and wooden Doric columns with, again, the unusual non-local feature of an entablature bearing triglyphs. To either side there are one-storied plastered brick wings, each with its own portico graced by two fluted columns; and pilasters at the ends of the façades—a feature never used externally in any of the pure Louisiana houses. The rather heavy and formal classic balustrades of the main part of the house are continued onto the parapets of the wings. The doorways and fanlights of the main building show excellent and definite Georgian influence. The whole ensemble is unlike anything we could find further down the Mississippi, though it has a special charm of its own.

And so, beneath the classic simplicity of the great stone urn, we find an echo of this simplicity in the pure contours of the house, contrasted as it is by the almost astonishing multiplicity in the surrounding plant world.

PLATE 48

THE HUB OF THE ROSE GARDEN

Rosedown Plantation (1835)

THE true glory of Rosedown, it would seem, is its gardens; among the loveliest in the South of the nineteenth century; and which now, when they can no longer receive all their former care, have a profuse and entangled beauty beggaring words. They comprise five acres to each side of the great alley. Daniel Turnbull and his wife, while in Europe, engaged the services of a Parisian landscape gardener—a disciple of the famed André L'Norte, who composed the gardens of Versailles—to design those at Rosedown. Everywhere there are winding paths outlined by box hedges. And everywhere there is a living vibrant blaze of color—a veritable feast of scent—roses, jasmine, sweet olive, lavender, azaleas, lilies, camellias. Among trees, there is even the cryptomeria, one of the sacred trees of Japan.

Its furniture, and its library, are probably the next two most distinctive features of Rosedown. In the hexagonal entrance hall there is the original Longfellow pattern wall paper, lit, at one time, with bronze chandeliers fitted with whale oil lamps. Elsewhere are black Carrara marble mantels, andirons of hammered brass, crimson brocade draperies, hand-painted linen shades, a grand piano designed for Rosedown by Jonas Chickering; rosewood furniture by Prudence Mallard and François Seignouret of New Orleans. Here, too, are oil portraits by the Philadelphia painter, Thomas Sully; and a portrait of Eliza Pirrie, the beauty, by John James Audubon in 1822. In the library are rare books, contemporary with the house; old sets of Shakespeare, portfolios of engravings, an Elephant Edition of Audubon's *Birds of America*—all contained in mahogany cases made in France for this room.

Leaving all this, we pass once more to the grounds where, at the heart of the rose garden, is a beautiful little garden house; its sides latticed, its *pigeonnier*-like roof terminating in a finial. Through its archways—which we see opposite—we can wander, it may be, into a timeless spring. . . .

The hours, indeed, passed slowly here—each laden with a sense of a myriad mute memories; the sad changes of men, in time. . . . And the modern world begins to seem almost a nightmare, too foreboding and remote to be real; too much like the fancies our minds create in fever. . . .

PLATE 49
THE FIGURE OF NORTH AMERICA
Rosedown Plantation (1835)

BUT we must not forget yet another unique feature of Rosedown. In addition to the rows of mythological figures paralleling the trees of the avenue, there is a shorter transverse line of statues facing the house. These represent the various continents of the world and were also, it is said, brought from Europe. They must have been created especially for Rosedown. Among these is the figure seen opposite—that of North America; which exhibits a special and charming kind of fantasy. A plump Indian maiden, clothed in feathers, and with a quiver holding arrows to her side, she stands with one foot on a miniature alligator. Over her right shoulder seems to be a lion skin; while her broken arm once held a cornucopia of Feliciana cotton bolls.

In this captivating fantasy is a quality as native to nineteenth century America as the wooden cigar-store Indian; and—it would be possible to contend—more indigenous to Louisiana, perhaps, than the house itself.

PLATE 50

THE LUMINOUS COLUMNS (NO. 8)

Oak Alley (Bon Séjour) Plantation (1832-1856)

BROTHER to the Josephine who became the mighty Valcour Aime's wife (see Plate 21), and brother, too, to the brilliant André Bienvenu Roman who became Governor of Louisiana at the age of thirty-five, Jacques Télesphore Roman III erected the house called originally Bon Séjour. Before the site already grew a twin line of oaks, planted by some anonymous French pioneer in, it is said, the 1690's. Here, too, stood the small colonial structure which this adventurous first settler—who planned the oaks better than he knew—erected in the wilderness. It was demolished before the new structure was started—which was in 1832. Brick kilns were constructed on the plantation, the swamps were raided for cypress by the slaves. Four years were required; but when finished, it was in the finest Louisiana Classic style.

Jacques Roman built this house partly because of his beautiful and discriminating wife, Josephine Pilié, descended from Santo Domingo refugees. It was she who chose the name of the house, and the Romans, indeed, were to know many hours of rest and happiness here. Travellers passing on the busy traffic of the Mississippi, unaccustomed to the soft and appropriate French designation, began to call the place, simply, Oak Alley.

The Civil War ruined the Roman family, as it did so many others. A family named Sobral—from the tropics—held the house during the Reconstruction Period. But finally, they too left and Oak Alley faced the elements alone. Moss swept its gray deadening waves over the trees of the alley, the marble figures and urns struggled with vines and weeds and finally disappeared; owls and bats found harbor in mouldering chambers; the roof opened up. But Bon Séjour did not belie its name—it was more fortunate than most. Towards 1914 Mr. and Mrs. Jefferson D. Hardin, Jr. bought the plantation; and it was they who saved the building by repairing its roof and windows. In 1925, Mr. and Mrs. Andrew Stewart acquired the estate, and decided upon a complete restoration, which was done by the firm of Armstrong and Koch. Oak Alley became thus the first of the great Louisiana plantation houses to be restored.

As we see it now, in the opposing picture, the gigantic limbs of the oaks, like enormous tentacles, flow horizontally past the light pure verticals of the pillars. There is a dramatic contrast between the columns of man and those of nature; a beautiful interplay of the irregular and rhythmic dark with sharp luminous whites, while the pyramid of elephant-ear leaves below supports the base of the composition. Towards the center left of the picture, at a place where a diseased oak branch has had to be removed, appears a face somewhat reminiscent of a Maori war mask—perhaps imprinted here by a phantom from the dark days of the house—days which now seem departed forever.

PLATE 51

THE ENSHADOWED PILLARS (NO. 6)

Oak Alley (Bon Séjour) Plantation (1832-1836)

DESPITE some popular misconceptions, George Swainey was the original architect for Bon Séjour. Seventy feet square, the house follows closely, but not mechanically, the Louisiana Classic plan—a great central hall, repeated on the second floor, and even in the attic; four rooms arranged to either side of the halls; a brick verandah almost level with the earth, the roof hipped, and bearing a roof deck, and three dormer windows to each side. Here is a triumph of brick and cypress wood. The oft-repeated minor note of Georgian appears in the fine doors with their fan transoms.

Noting that his great oaks numbered twenty-eight, Jacques Roman had the columns surrounding the house number the same; even the slave cabins to the rear repeated the magic number. The columns have been called Doric. Actually, a close study of their details—the fillet, taurus, echinus, etc.—reveals them to be something between Roman Doric and Tuscan. It is this customary lack, in most of the Louisiana Classic houses, of close adherence to any fixed order, which was one of the elements—though not the most important one—in shaping the indigenous quality of the Louisiana Classic style. But it revealed an important tendency—the willingness and vision to modify accepted treatment to meet local needs, or the special demands of the specific material used.

Unfortunately, the *garconnières* to either side of the house have disappeared; so, too, have most of the auxiliary buildings—save two in the rear—one now used as a guest house, the other for the plantation manager.

When looking towards the rear of the house, as we do in Plate 51, we cannot fail to appreciate how beautifully the delicate bluish-green of the simple wooden railing of the gallery— repeated as it is, by the blinds of the long French windows—blends with the plastered brick walls, suffused with a rose pink. It is as though a warmth has dwelt here always, and not even the gray things of the most extreme shadow have ever been able to make it depart.

PLATE 52

TITANIC ARCADE

Oak Alley (Bon Séjour) Plantation (1832-1836)

IN Plate 52 we are looking from the house towards the levee, the full three hundred yards of the great oak alley. Beside us, the huge pillars of the house, eight feet in circumference, are enwreathed by ivy; others bear honeysuckle and Cherokee roses. The flashing blades of the Spanish Dagger and the palmettoes, the green mist-like foliage of parkinsonias, the quivering sail-like leaves of banana trees filled with light blowing from the sun, the tight delicate little blossoms of the crepe myrtles—all these, and more, are about us; set in a scented frame of nearly five hundred rose bushes, innumerable lilies, jessamine, and other blooms.

Before us stretches the arcade which once, during the Roman occupation, had a driveway of clam shells bordered by a walk of brick—now a verdant and enormous carpet. Above are the superb arboreal architectonics of the oaks, each tree with a spread of about 150 feet, and meeting in a mighty arch above the alley. Sunbeams, falling like great spotlights through the million murmuring leaves, create illusory effects of a titanic stage—a stage which would have delighted such masters of theatrical magnificence as the seventeenth century Bibiena family.

As the light moves lower, and shadows creep longer across the avenue, we know that minutes, even hours, mean nothing here. We are in the presence of the oaks; and they came before us and all our works. They will last after we are gone. We linger—in the golden time-haunted light—no more able to stir, it seems, than a fly in amber. And if we are fortunate enough, we stay till the sun dies in a lonely fanfare of flame through the great trees, now black elemental giants expressing all the tremendous strength of the earth. And in the moonlight, when it comes in silver softness, the leaves whisper things no human tongue can ever translate; and the scents of the gardens cause the mind to be thronged by evanescent phantoms of impossible happiness. And in this spell we are rapt, for an interval we could not ever really measure, from all our bonds of care. . . .

PLATE 53

THE GUARDIAN

Oak Alley (Bon Séjour) Plantation (1832-1836)

IN this plate we have an extreme diagonal view of the front of Oak Alley, accentuating the mighty colonnade. A huge yucca plant (or Spanish Dagger as it is called in Louisiana) with its many-bladed form, stands like a guardian beside the corner of the house; its daggers brandished brightly and fiercely in the sun. . . .

It has been mentioned that Jacques Roman repeated the number of the oaks in his great alley in the columns of his house. But the numerical duplication was but an incidental expression of a more significant and subtle process, perhaps, which occurred simultaneously, and upon whose implications the careful observer cannot help but ponder. It was as though the natural majesty and massiveness of the oaks were transposed into the pillars; and as though the pillars grew by a process analogous to that of the mighty trees; so that here—and in all other of the best Louisiana plantation houses as well—the natural landscape re-appeared in the psychological landscape and this, in turn, influenced the nature of the architecture. In a very real sense this complex transposition is one of the secrets of the indigenous quality of the finest Louisiana plantation architecture. The giants of the forest were repeated in the colonnades; the lightness and spaciousness of the great encircling galleries were, in a certain sense, fashioned by the very air, and as though they invited the elements; in the vast linear area of the houses in proportion to their height, and in the never entirely absent feeling of powerful horizontals—the wide flat terrain of Louisiana was echoed. All of these things gave the houses a feeling of being direct organic outgrowths of their environment. . . .

From the first of the well-known Spring Fiestas of New Orleans, Oak Alley has never failed to be included. Throngs visit it each year, knowing they will find here an important part of Louisiana's past; which has taken on, by what seems almost a miracle, a new lease on life.

PLATE 54

THE WINTER OF ABANDONMENT

Bocage Plantation (1801-1840)

BOCAGE is another house erected by the great Bringier family, who built The Hermitage (Plate 41) and the even more famous White Hall. Marius Pons Bringier, head of the family, presented this house, in 1801 it is said, to his daughter Françoise—then fourteen years old—as a wedding gift. Her husband, Christophe Colomb, then thirty-one, was quite a remarkable character. In France he had belonged to the class which helped bring on the French Revolution. Fleeing to Santo Domingo he found himself, shortly, amid another social upheaval —this time the slaves—and came to America in 1795. It was not long after his arrival in Louisiana that he found himself being entertained by the Bringiers. He was an adventurer, but in addition, he had all the social graces—he was a good musician, dancer, vocalist—and he was wealthy. Françoise and Christophe—the latter disinclined towards labor—found a somewhat unusual, but as it turned out, a quite happy pattern of life. Françoise directed the work in the cane fields and sugar mill, and saw that Christophe's wants were met; Christophe, for his part, played music brilliantly, entertained the company at their social gatherings, and had built for himself a delightful boat, equipped with tinted sails and a fringed silken canopy. In this, reclining on his cushions, and rowed by his slaves, he went along the bayous, visiting the numerous relatives and friends, while composing verses for his dear wife. Lest those who adhere to the mistaken concept that all poets are effeminate feel that here they have found another example— it must be said that Christophe was quite able to take care of himself, and did, on those occasions when he felt it necessary to do so. Among such occasions were several in which his descent from the French branch of the family of Christopher Columbus, America's discoverer, was questioned. Françoise and Christophe were happy together, despite all odds, for more than two score of years.

The house itself was two-storied, square, and with a very unusual arrangement for its eight plastered brick columns supporting the heavy entablature. They were square, six of them heavy, but the two central ones rather thin, and set close to the adjoining pillars. There were the usual wide central halls. In the 1840's much remodeling took place—interior decorations in Empire style were added, a magnificent double folding door on the second floor, a floor of black and white diamond tiles below.

But the lean years came; and the house, abandoned, became occupied by squatters. Finally, at the time this picture was made (in Feb. 1938) the roof had fallen in, and the upper floor. And winter had come; the winter not merely of season, but the winter of neglect and ruin. The house seemed to radiate the cold of human untenancy—an effect heightened by the bare stiff arch of the tree limb against the cold gray of the wintry sky.

Some years ago, this house appeared in a section of the Farm Security Administration documentary film "The River" directed by Pare Lorentz.

But now, a new phase in what seemed the dying life of the house has begun. Under the recent ownership of Dr. E. G. Kohlsdorf and his wife, the former Dr. Anita Crozat, it is being restored by means of some of the most modern techniques yet used on any of the houses—the walls, newly insulated, will be more capable than they were originally of withstanding the climate. Stronger than ever, Bocage will be able to face the years.

PLATE 55

THE ENSHADOWED PILLARS (NO. 7)

René Beauregard (Bueno Retiro) Plantation (1840)

WITHIN the area of the Battlefield of New Orleans, there still stands the crumbling mass of the René Beauregard House—once known as Bueno Retiro, or Sweet Seclusion. The elder Gallier designed it in 1840 for the Marquis de Trava, a Spanish nobleman who was his friend. During the Reconstruction years it passed from a second owner, J. A. Fernandez, to Judge René Beauregard, eldest son of General Pierre G. T. Beauregard, the Creole military leader of the Confederacy who, in the 1880's, could be seen playing with his grandchildren in its gardens. The house then had an approach of more than two hundred yards, hedged with Bengal roses to either side, and the surrounding grounds landscaped.

Architecturally, the house forms another important step in the evolution of Louisiana architecture from the original Colonial style. The great cement-covered brick columns which supplanted the original squattish brick columns below and wooden colonettes above, and then appeared in a single colonnade, are here presented at the next stage of development—a second identical colonnade was created at the rear of the house. The floor plan is that of the second stage, however: three rooms wide, and one deep, with a hall absent. All the rooms, front and rear, open onto the galleries. In the attic the beams are all pegged; and by means of some excellent brick masonry, the flues all merge into two huge chimneys. The staircase was inside and at the south end of the house. Later, there were two wings—only one of which still stood at the time of the opposite picture—and this one was definitely added at a date later than the other. Our view has been so made as to avoid showing this later wing, and so to convey something of the original appearance of the building.

The coloring of René Beauregard was excellent—a deep orange for the walls; a soft deep blue for the shutters, beams, and ceilings; the slates (later) browns and purples; earthy reds for the bricks of the verandah; grayish white for the columns and trim.

And so, in the long sad light of sunset, we gaze at the tall and stately pillars of Sweet Seclusion—pillars on which the leaves of pecan and oak print designs more ancient still than the house itself, designs that evoke the loneliness and dismay of years beyond recall. . . .

PLATE 56

BENEATH THE RAIN OF THE MOSS

The Houmas House (Burnside Plantation) (1800-1840)

IN 1812 General Wade Hampton (of Revolutionary War fame) purchased from Daniel Clark a tract of land once possessed by the Houmas Indians; and which, for many years to come, was to become a stronghold of non-Creole wealth and influence in Louisiana. Except for occasional visits, however, the Hamptons continued to reside in their Carolina home. But in 1840 the General's daughter, Caroline, married John Smith Preston, also a Carolinian, and they came to take over the Hampton properties in Louisiana. It was then that the main part of the present house was erected. The Prestons stayed for a while, but finally went away. The call of their Carolina was too strong, and in 1857 they sold the estate, then ten thousand acres, to John Burnside for a sum said to approach two million dollars. Burnside, coming from Ireland, as a youth had been informally adopted by Andrew Bierne, a wealthy Virginian. Bierne set Burnside up in business in New Orleans, and the Irishman, about whose life there still hover some unsolved questions, quickly became one of the leading merchants. In time, at Burnside, he became also one of the largest sugar planters in the United States. In his sumptuous house he led the life of a prince—not even the Civil War disturbed him greatly. When General Ben Butler decided to appropriate the house, Burnside, as a British subject, faced him down, and won. Burnside collected plantations around—the Bringiers, the deceased Valcour Aime, and his holdings rose to over twenty thousand acres. An Englishman, visiting the house in 1861, looked forth from its belvedere and called the view—with its great fields of cane and corn, its four sugar houses, its miles of roads and drainage ditches, its slave village—one of the most striking of its kind in the world.

In 1881 Burnside died, unmarried, and his plantation returned to the family that had befriended him—the Biernes. Through a daughter of the Biernes, who became the wife of William Porcher Miles, president of South Carolina College, it had once more a new owner. Colonel Miles (he had also been on Beauregard's staff) knew nothing of sugar-cane culture. But he could learn, and did. He studied the sugar experiments of Valcour Aime, he formed a company, and in time, was producing, amazingly enough, twenty million pounds of sugar per year. Meanwhile, he built up one of the finest libraries in the South.

Upon his death in 1899, the properties passed to his son, Dr. William Porcher Miles, Jr. who held them till 1940, when the house alone was purchased by Dr. George B. Crozat of New Orleans. And thus, for the first time in over one hundred years, a Creole family once more possess this mighty house.

PLATE 57

THE SOLID PHANTOM

The Houmas House (Burnside Plantation) (1800-1840)

LONG before the present house was erected, another house, in the early Colonial style, stood on these grounds, sometime around 1800. It was used, it is said, by one of the Bringiers, and later, occasionally, by the Hamptons. When the Prestons erected the present house in 1840, they did not destroy the older structure, as was usually the case in most such instances. Instead, they incorporated it in the rear of the new house (see right side of Plate 56), leaving an arcade which became a porte-cochère. In the new house the traditional Louisiana style was not entirely predominant, however, for they remembered well the manor houses of the East. There are traces of Atlantic seaboard influence—notably in the glassed belvedere—but not as strongly, of course, as at Rosedown (Plate 47) and Greenwood (Plate 42). Nevertheless, tradition came back to its own in the plastered brick Tuscan columns, so massive and majestic; in the wide central halls, above and below; in the arrangement of the four enormous rooms to each floor; and in the two exceedingly fine hexagonal brick *garçonnières*—well placed to the sides of the house. It is one of these we see in Plate 57; its exquisitely soft lines radiant in the light; the moss drapes swaying like a curtain, half-revealing, half-concealing, this glimpse of a structure which seems to rise like a materialized phantom from the very heart of Louisiana's past.

Having acquired the house, Dr. George B. Crozat, working through the firm of Freret and Wolf, proceeded to a task of love—the task of restoring Houmas House to its original condition. Among other things, the ornamental balustrades, placed along the parapets and around the belvedere by the over-lush taste of the 1890's were wisely removed; and much effort and expense were incurred in the effort to restore the entablature to the simplicity it possessed in the 1840's.

This task recently completed, it can be said that no more magnificent restoration has been effected among Louisiana's old houses in the last several years than this. Houmas House, in its new incarnation, (Plate 56) emerges, resplendent, in its soft wavering frame of gray moss and glittering leaves. An incomparable serenity dwells here still; as though, by natural right, it has dwelt here forever. . . .

PLATE 58

VICTORIAN STILL LIFE

The Houmas House (Burnside Plantation) (1800-1840)

DR. MILES was still in possession of Houmas House when the adjoining picture was made, in 1938. The attics alone of the house are large enough for several families; and the objects seen were within one of the side dormers. The graceful and fantastic oil lamps, the plaster statuette of Venus, were arranged in a pattern suggestive of the crowded ornateness of Victorian life, its wry charm and perverse fantasy. The sole light was that of the dusty window. Yet an effect of soft and subtle sunlight without glare—very difficult under the circumstances—has been conveyed.

Since occupation of the house by the Crozat family, much of the magnificent furniture from their New Orleans residence has been moved out to Houmas House. It is no exaggeration to say that the house now contains some of the most superb furniture that can be found, at the present time, in any of the restored houses.

PLATE 59

THE MAGNIFICENT SPIRAL (NO. 1)

The Houmas House (Burnside Plantation) (1800-1840)

IN 1938, too, the picture opposite was composed. We are shown the breathtakingly beautiful upward swirl of the staircase, one of the finest in Louisiana. Perhaps only such a magnificent staircase as that in the Bradish Johnston House, or in the old Campbell Mansion in New Orleans, or that in the plantation structure known as Afton Villa (see Plate 76), where the spiral is less sweeping, can now be compared to this. The slight irregularities in the railing are not photographic distortions. The stringer ornaments are restrained and chastely beautiful.

With supernal grace, the rhythm of the staircase ascends—a very poem in wood.

PLATE 60

THE BESIEGING WILDERNESS (NO. 1)

Ashland (Belle Hélène) Plantation (1841)

ASHLAND was another of the mighty works of the senior Gallier, greatest builder of Louisiana Classic architecture. It was erected in 1841 and became the home of Duncan Farrar Kenner, one of the wealthiest and most influential planters ever to appear in Louisiana, and who was to rise high in the councils of the Confederacy. Kenner combined the social graces of the Creoles with the energy and business acumen of the Americans, and his house, which he had built for the lovely and vivacious Nanine Bringier as a wedding present, became famous for its hospitality, its wine stock, its library, and its racing stable. Kenner, who was partly educated in France, who was a lover of books, of wine, and of horse flesh—laying out his own private race track near the house—made a fortune in sugar. And, mid-year in 1862, he made the far-sighted and revolutionary proposal to Jefferson Davis that the South free the slaves (he himself being one of the largest slave holders in the lower Mississippi valley) in order to offset the humane appeal of the ideology of the North, and in order to gain the help of France and England. Davis demurred, but in 1865, appointed him the Confederacy's minister pleni-potentiary to Europe, with powers to make this most necessary sacrifice in order to gain help. After a long and breathtaking series of adventures, Kenner managed to get through the Union blockade, only to arrive in Europe with the Confederate government tottering. It was too late. Kenner, however, lived to see the collapse of the cause his daring suggestion might have saved, had it been adopted in time; lived to see the decline of the majestic house at whose social functions had appeared all the notables of the day.

A house whose great walls (as we see them in Plate 60) are still completely encircled by rows of gigantic square pillars, without a single curvilinear element in any of their details; between whose colonnades fall the hot patterns of Louisiana sunlight, pitilessly revealing now a physiognomy of incredible age (Louisiana climate can often age buildings with more than twice the tempo of a more temperate climate), the tints of advanced decay. We see, too, how the house, despite its tremendous size is dwarfed by the enormous upsurge of the oaks surround-ing it—the former gardens having been reclaimed by the wilderness; while from above, from around, from everywhere, we see, and feel, the slow sad drip of the moss. And, after a while, this drip and its grayness seem to get into our blood; they steal the hues of things and give a funereal and disquieting cast to the whole land that not even the banana trees, with their great green sails of sun-seeking tissue, their marvelous liquid pouring of light from their translucent leaf surfaces, can wholly dispel. . . .

PLATE 61

THE BESIEGING WILDERNESS (NO. 2)

THIS is not Ashland Plantation, but another altogether different building. However, this plate represents an attempt to deal in an even more expressive way with such a contrast as is shown in Plate 60.

Here, the terrible and prolonged struggle between the plant forms, and the architectural forms, so characteristic of Louisiana, has been carried a step further, symbolically, by means of a double exposure. And we can sense something of the savage crowding of Louisiana vegetation, the violence of the plant life, accelerated by the heat and dampness; exhibiting itself in an amazing profusion of vegetable forms. While enveloping all this, the moss overspreads the trees like sinister cobwebs.

PLATE 62

THE MIGHTY PILLARS

Ashland (Belle Hélène) Plantation (1841)

ASHLAND was built with a monumentality never before equalled in Louisiana. The completely square columns are nearly four feet around, and thirty feet high, supporting an entablature proportionately heavy, the exceptional height of which bears only one ornament—a severely simple course of dentils. But though the columns set the note for this severity, no real harshness of line can be found anywhere despite all the apparently sharp verticals. In reality, soft richly crumbling surfaces and coloring everywhere modify this impression when we draw closer. Originally, the walls were tinted a light lemon, the shutters of the French widows greenish-blue, and the pillars and entablature, white. The thick walls are solid stuccoed brick, marked off to resemble stone; the galleries, of pine, are twenty feet wide; and below, the verandah was paved with brick and tile. Within, at the end of the huge central hall, is a flat spiral staircase, with solid cypress treads; and all the rooms were graced with marble mantels. The hipped roof was originally of slate, it is now of sheet metal.

At the time the opposite picture was made, in 1939, only two of Ashland's many outbuildings remained—a two-storied square *pigeonnier*, and a ruinous barn. Looking diagonally at the side of the house (as we are in Plate 62) an imposing portion of the gigantic quadrangle of Ashland faces us. Towards the rear, the house is crowded close by the damp, sinister and overhanging masses of tremendous oaks. Time was, when these foreboding trees were in a park; now the park has become a grove, grown savage and twilit. . . .

(News has been recently received that Ashland is to be restored by the Hayward family of Germania Plantation. This task, undoubtedly, will entail enormous labor and expense. The present Mrs. Hayward is a daughter of John B. Reuss, last previous owner of Ashland, under whom the house became known as Belle Hélène.)

PLATE 63

THE HEAD OF POWER

(The Tomb of Duncan Farrar Kenner)

IN the quiet and secluded old cemetery of Donaldsonville, not too far from his erstwhile great house, Duncan Farrar Kenner is buried. He died in 1887, at the age of seventy-four. Not far from him, in another of the vaults of the same massive tomb, lies Nanine, his wife, daughter of the Bringiers, who played so large a part in Louisiana plantation history. His tomb is one of the simple vaults we see squared off on the face of the huge raised tomb of the Bringier family. And it is inscribed, with equal simplicity, *Inter Pares Dux* (Leader Among his Peers).

Duncan Kenner was an admirer of Henry Clay, protagonist of those who favored wealth and privilege. He even named his house after Clay's home in Kentucky. Kenner, himself, became the symbol of power in the South. And now, the great draped urn surmounting the tomb, like the terrible and empty head of power, looks away—looks over the massed green of the trees, the soft clouds, the wide earth—where power endures for so little a while. . . .

PLATE 64

ON LAFOURCHE'S BANKS

Belle Alliance Plantation (1846)

ON the verdant banks of Bayou Lafourche—one of Louisiana's richest regions—there stands a house which seems to have been one of the few which escaped pillage during the Civil War. A minor military engagement, however, seems to have occurred on its grounds, but with no damage to the house itself. The present house was built by Charles Kock— wealthy descendant of an ancient Dutch family—in 1846, on the site of an earlier house destroyed by fire. Kock had not only a magnificent town house in New Orleans (known as Marble House) but he maintained an establishment in Paris as well. However, Belle Alliance was not merely a manor—it was an active plantation too, and produced an exceptionally fine grade of sugar.

The house combines the massive dignity of the Louisiana Classic houses with, towards its side elevations, the lightness characteristic of the iron balconies of the Vieux Carré though, of course, its pillars are not as massive as those of Ashland (Plate 62). There is, in its raised basement effect, its wide exterior stair, a hint, too, of those wilderness cottages, earliest of all Louisiana houses, which were raised on piers a full floor above the marshy earth. The main floor gallery is extended to the sides of the house, where it becomes enclosed, and partly covered, by light iron railings and canopies. At present, the house has thirty-two rooms, twelve on each of its floors, and eight in the two-storied rear wing, which was added later.

Its gardens were noted for their camellias; its pigeon houses were covered with wisteria and honeysuckle; there was also, a marble fountain, with urns and statuary. It remained in the hands of the Kock family till 1915, when, after several transfers, it became the property of Mr. and Mrs. C. S. Churchill, who have furnished its magnificent central hall—with its roseate plaster and its stained glass skylight—as well as its lovely rooms, with fine antiques. The exterior of the house has been somewhat marred by screens added for insect protection. But as we see it from a distance, so well does it borrow its tints from its surroundings, that it reposes in perfect harmony.

PLATE 65

THE MINATORY ARM

Bellechasse Plantation (-1846)

THE name of Bellechasse is interwoven with that of Judah P. Benjamin, statesman of the Confederacy, who started life as a notarial clerk but whose legal talents, eventually, were recognized by two continents. Strangely enough, this brilliant man of Jewish extraction, became one of the greatest defenders of the economic and social concepts of the Creoles, and of the men of the South, in general. He served Louisiana in the U. S. Senate from 1853 to 1861, was the Confederate Secretary of State, and after the collapse of the Jefferson Davis regime, fled to England, where he became an exile. In England, he rose to the highest prominence, becoming counselor to Queen Victoria. He died in Paris in 1884.

It was in 1844 that he purchased property belonging to William C. Milne, down the west bank of the river from New Orleans. The house then standing on the property was demolished in 1846 and the Bellechasse we know today, was erected near its site.

The house is a huge square three-storied building. It has twenty enormous rooms, central halls 16 feet wide, and a winding mahogany staircase. There is a lower, as well as an upper, gallery; also tall square columns—all of cypress. The house, during Benjamin's ownership, was noted for its munificent social affairs; and was filled with fine furniture and objects of art. All these were stripped from the house during the Union occupation of New Orleans. Falling into ruin, it has, at least, been saved from the river, by being moved back on two occasions. In this process, unfortunately, it has lost some of its fine interior finish.

For some years, restoration of the house has been planned by the Judah P. Benjamin Memorial Association. These plans, however, have been held up by the recent War, and by lack of sufficient funds.

Looking at the house from the rear, as it is presented to us in Plate 65, we see how the leafless tree stretches its aged and threatening arm—the very arm of disaster—towards the structure. Let us hope that Bellechasse, too, will not fall victim to the years.

PLATE 66

THE LUMINOUS COLUMNS (NO. 3)

Madewood Plantation (1844-1848)

LED on by the glowing tales they had read in a contemporary book of the glories of Louisiana, the first of the Pugh family, leaving their North Carolina home, arrived in the region of the Bayou Teche around 1818. Shortly, there were three brothers—Augustin, Thomas, and Dr. Whitmell H. Pugh—as well as the latter's nine-year-old son—William W. Pugh. Conditions on the Teche being unsatisfactory, they moved to the richer agricultural section of Bayou Lafourche, and proceeded to amass enormous wealth, and in time, to establish a dynasty.

In the 1830's old Dr. W. H. Pugh's son erected Woodlawn (Plate 93). Not to be outdone, Thomas, the youngest of the three brothers, decided he would have a house, too. But it was to take some time—longer than he thought. First, though, he married. His wife was Eliza Foley, daughter of one of the two English-speaking families who had arrived in the Lafourche region before the Pughs. This was to establish a tradition. For the Pughs were never to intermarry with any of their Latin neighbors, mostly descendants of those unfortunate Acadians driven from Canada by the British, although they got along with them quite well. Eliza, too, wanted a great house. Four years were spent, it is said, cutting the lumber and making the bricks; then four more years in erecting the house. This is not too surprising when we consider its construction (see Plate 67). But in 1848 it was completed. Shortly before this happened, Thomas, tragically, fell victim to the current yellow fever epidemic. Eliza, quite capably, carried on, seeing the job through to its hasty end. Since all the very large amount of wood used in the building had originated on the plantation itself, the house was called Madewood. The structure stood forth, a thing of beauty at which all the bayou people could marvel.

Madewood weathered the War years well. Due to Eliza's tact and shrewdness, it was left untouched by the Union troops. And it remained in the hands of the Pughs until 1916, when Mr. and Mrs. R. L. Baker acquired it. Once more Madewood was fortunate. Its new owners gave it all the care it deserved, and had been getting through the years. In 1946 Madewood passed to its present owner, Mr. Bronier Thibaut—long a resident of the section. And thus, still another non-Creole stronghold goes back to the Latins. Mr. Thibaut has immediately proceeded to give the house the moderate amount of repair necessary. Madewood is one of the few Louisiana plantation houses which, during its entire existence, has been neither prettified for tourists, nor allowed to be overwhelmed by age and neglect.

In Plate 66 we behold the house as it was in 1939. Against the splendor of the Ionic columns in the evening light, we see the rich dark mass of the live oak, thickened with its burden of shadow and moss.

PLATE 67

MOON OVER MADEWOOD

Madewood Plantation (1844-1848)

MADEWOOD departed further than its nearest neighbor, Woodlawn (Plate 93), from the Louisiana Classic tradition. Instead of the low-pitched hipped roof, a finely proportioned pediment, lifting the roof high, appears. The columns, instead of springing from the earth, or from small pedestals—now are arranged on a stylobate as in a Greek temple. The usual Tuscan or Roman Doric pillars are supplanted by Greek Ionic ones, beautifully treated. And the *garçonnières* are replaced by two wings, whose outlines repeat in miniature those of the main building. These wings bear simple pilasters at their corners (again, quite unusually). and were originally connected to the house by flat-roofed passages. Each of these wings extends backwards—one, more than the length of the house; the other has never been completed according to plan. The left wing contains the service rooms, as well as a large ballroom. Altogether, this house could have appeared easily in Virginia or North Carolina.

The structure of Madewood is excellent. The stuccoed brick walls are from 18″ to 24″ thick; partition walls are 18″ all the way to the attics, where there are beams of heart cypress, 14″ on the square. The heavy walls contain more than sixty thousand bricks, it is said. There are some twenty rooms within. The interior of the house is notable for two massive halls, (above and below) whose further ends, immediately beyond the finely designed staircase, are rounded, and terminate in two sets of beautifully carved wooden Corinthian columns. The architect was Henry Howard, who later built another magnificent house, Nottaway.

Though the Pughs afterwards became great sugar planters, their fortunes began with cotton. In Plate 67 we not only see the house as it is now—but above it is a cotton moon; a moon which is, actually, a silver memento from the Cotton Centennial Exposition of 1884 in New Orleans. Its curlicued embellishments contrast admirably with the stark purity of the lines of the house. Fleecy clouds surround it, like wisps of cotton. Untroubled and lustrous, it shines over a house which, perhaps more than any other in Louisiana, has been able to survive the years untroubled. Long may it shine!

PLATE 68

THE WATERS OF MEMORY

Madewood Plantation (1844-1848)

AND now, through the magic of the camera, we plunge into the refreshing and lustrous waters of memory. We plunge, as through great dark veils of time, into a world we all once knew, a world we all seek, sporadically, to rediscover—the world of our childhood, the world of all lost years.

And we find a house, a bright and resplendent habitation, which is not only an enchanted synthesis of all our mingled and multiformed remembrances of the loveliest and most cherished places we have known; but also, the very living symbol of our myriad search, our devious questing and constant loss, our fevered and persistent resumption of seeking again—for a true and final home in the dark and troubled chaos of the modern world.

PLATE 69

IN SORROWFUL LIGHT (NO. 1)

Uncle Sam Plantation (1843-1849)

PERHAPS the three greatest single tragedies of plantation culture in our time are the claiming of Uncle Sam Plantation by the river, the demolition of Woodlawn, and the lapse of Belle Grove into irretrievable ruin—all of whose fates well exemplify the destruction left behind by the tremendous tread of time and social change in the lower Mississippi valley.

Uncle Sam was the last of the great truly Louisiana style (i.e. Louisiana Classic) houses to be built. Those which were to come after—Belle Grove, Afton Villa, San Francisco, Orange Grove—were to depart far from the indigenous feeling which had, till that time, developed so magnificently in Louisiana.

Surrounded by lanes of great oaks, enwound by a gigantic curve in the mighty Mississippi, at once mysterious and massive, the multi-pillared bulk of Uncle Sam dominated the countryside for close on to a century. Completed in 1849, on the site of a still earlier house destroyed by fire, it was erected by Pierre Auguste Samuel Fagot—the heart of a huge plantation lying near Convent, Louisiana, on the east bank of the river.

It was during these times that the high water mark in wealth accumulated from sugar was reached—many, and diverse, were the forms that gave expression to this wealth; the means of expression, it need hardly be added, sometimes fantastically tinged by the effects the special character of the Lousiana environment had on the imaginations of the planters. For instance, it was within this decade that Charles Durande, owner of Pine Alley Plantation near St. Martinville, had the fantastic wedding event recounted opposite Plate 34. It was during these days, too, that the luxury packets plied the broad Mississippi—the Natchez, the Robert E. Lee, the Eclipse, and others—and they all, at various times, knew the wharves of Uncle Sam. And, finally, it was between 1830 and 1845 that important improvements in the processing of sugar were introduced—thus making possible the rise of further great fortunes.

On a substructure of wealth amassed from sugar the great walls and pillars of Uncle Sam arose; pillars and walls whose golden-brown tint due, it is said, to the river sand used in the cement and mortar, lasted through all the years of their existence; and, with a strange symbolism, was not unlike the color of the "yellow" sugar which, antedating the final development of the refining process, formed, economically, their ultimate foundations.

Samuel Fagot, it seems, was, at the beginning—when, prior to 1830, he settled with his wife and two small daughters on the land which was later to be the plantation—no more than a small planter, supposedly of Breton origin, certainly not of any great affluence. He was, legend recounts, a thin dark-skinned man, with a black beard. But fortune conspired, and he had shrewdness and some imagination—he rode the rising tide of wealth. Small piece by piece, he acquired the land that was to become Uncle Sam Plantation. As his wealth grew, his imagination expanded. He saw the fine houses of his neighbors, the delicate furniture brought from Europe; and something of the desire to secure those things without which the possession of all the wealth in the world is hollow, the things that give meaning and pause to toil—must have overcome him.

And so, in the early 1840's he began his house. By slave labor, and from huge cypress

PLATE 70 THE MASSIVE COLUMNS

Uncle Sam Plantation (1843-1849)

timbers cut out of the swamps, and with countless bricks manufactured on the spot from river clay, he constructed it. Nearly six years of work, and the sum of $100,000 were expended in its erection. Furniture was imported from Europe, costing nearly as much again as the house itself. Today, the house possibly could not be duplicated for less than a half-million dollars, if any amount of money could secure cypress of the size used in this building—plaster work, and furniture, of equal quality.

The main structure—two-storied and tremendous in scale—had a hipped and dormered roof supported on all sides by huge Roman Doric columns, twenty-eight in number (see Plate 70). Its plan remained true to Louisiana Classic tradition; the great central halls above and below, the four rooms on each floor opening into the halls, and opening, as well, onto the broad encircling gallery and verandah by means of their long windows. Surrounding the house, and in perfect scale, were six other structures (all one-storied save the *Pigeonniers*)—two *garçonnières*, one to either side; two smaller buildings to the rear—one a kitchen, kept separate from the main house as a safeguard from fire—the other, the plantation office; and flanking these, two hexagonal *pigeonniers*—originally intended as dovecotes. The kitchen and office, alone among the buildings, bore pediments, and were like small Greek temples strayed, somehow, into Louisiana; but built of materials unlike anything the Greeks themselves would have used—cypress wood and brick, so that they exuded the feeling of being miniature temples to a misplaced past (see Plate 71). All of these buildings, nevertheless, had the same basic architectural treatment, and embodied an intense simplicity and a massive dignity. The yard to the rear of the kitchen and office, with its twin *pigeonniers* and their pointed roofs, breathed the spirit of provincial France—a France which actually lived in America till 1940 (see Plate 72).

Everywhere feeling for the innate qualities of the materials available was shown, though Fagot, who was not an architect, must himself have designed the house. Everywhere the inherent character of the building materials used was stressed—the fine stark use of cypress in the entablatures bringing out the beauty of the wood; the excellent proportioning of the columns and walls in terms of brick; the slow careful workmanship throughout. Its materials gathered from the very soil in which it had its roots, the house rose slowly, like a great organic growth; becoming a perfect expression of the Louisiana of its time and place.

Far beyond the main group of buildings were the orchards; aligned to each side of these were forty cabins for the many slaves; and finally, further still, came the fields of cane, the barns, and the great sugar mill. This last structure, when sold, with its antiquated machinery, for $10,000 during the 1930's, brought its buyer, when demolished, more than that sum, it is said, from the sale of the bricks alone.

It was in this great house, then, that Samuel Fagot accumulated a vast fortune in sugar. And it was here that, outgrowing his former economical mode of existence, life was lived with a lavishness and hospitality legendary even in the old South. Some of the visitors, it may be added, loved both wine and cards; and the *garçonnières* of Uncle Sam, it has been hinted, saw more money change hands than any other of the Louisiana of that day. Despite all this, however,

PLATE 71   TEMPLE TO A MISPLACED PAST

Uncle Sam Plantation (1843-1849)

Fagot himself seems to have retained, through the years, the original simplicity of his personal needs. Then, too, there was about him something of austerity, tempered with gentleness that showed itself in his treatment of his numerous youthful relatives, whose familiar appellation, "Uncle Sam's place," probably gave the house its name, and, as well, his slaves, for whom he provided both a church and a hospital. But to the end—his death came shortly before the outbreak of the Civil War—Samuel Fagot remained the vital spark at the heart of this huge plantation; the man through whose single life poured multiple living currents from the lives of the numerous slaves, the countless visitors, the plentiful relatives, the myriad existences of growing and moving things—the great green waves of the cane, the crystalline tide of the processed sugar, the ripening fruit of the trees, the thick flood of the Mississippi, the ships that bore the culture of France, the seeds of ideas—integrating all these things into one sentient whole; a man who never knew the dead world of numerals, of paper profits—who knew only, and always, the life of the earth, the riches of the soil; who could sense, directly and immediately, the meaning of wealth.

With Samuel Fagot's death, management of the plantation passed to Lucien Malus, husband of Félicie—one of Samuel Fagot's two daughters—under whose direction the plantation managed to weather the Reconstruction period.

Lucien and Félicie Malus, in turn, had two daughters, who married two brothers, Jules and Camile Jacobs. The Jacobs brothers, too, were energetic and succeeded in retaining some measure of prosperity at the plantation despite what was happening coincidentally elsewhere. They were, for example, the first planters in that part of Louisiana to use tractors on a large scale. Some of the same machinery they introduced, abandoned and rusty, remained on the broad verandahs of the main house during its last days. Plate 69 with its luminous gray tones, conveys something of the special melancholy of the house towards the close of its life. Notwithstanding their efforts, however, the far reaching results of the economic twilight following the Civil War, together with the later and as disastrous effects due to competition from increased foreign production of sugar, and, also, disease of the cane itself, could not, finally, be evaded.

PLATE 72   TRANSPLANTED FRANCE

Uncle Sam Plantation (1843-1849)

About 1915, Jules Jacobs sold the plantation to a New Orleans commission merchant—and the great house then had seen its final days of human occupancy—there being no one who could afford keeping it in proper condition.

Meanwhile, the river, silent and implacable, had been creeping ever closer, drawing its coils tighter about the house, undermining the upstream side of the bend enclosing the plantation. Successive levee set-backs had to take place. With them went the fine lawns, the wharves, the oak alleys. At length, in the spring of 1940, the ultimate blow was struck. The U. S. Engineers, in charge of all levee construction and protection along the Mississippi River, determined that still another set-back must be made, if a levee failure was to be avoided. And so, demolition of Uncle Sam, of all its buildings, was commenced. At the time of its destruction, it was probably the most complete plantation group left in the entire South. Ironically enough, on March 12 of that year, the U. S. Engineer Office in New Orleans received the following telegram from the Director of the National Park Service in Washington:

> Have learned of the impending demolition of the Uncle Sam Plantation near Convent, Louisiana. Stop. Can demolition be deferred short time pending investigation by National Park Service to determine possibilities for status as a national monument or historic site?

It was then too late. The house was three quarters gone—its massive walls, with their irreplaceable materials and workmanship, smashed and torn into heaps of rubble. Thus, on a bitter concluding note, ends the history of Uncle Sam—lost in the slow sullen waters of the Mississippi, its site engulfed in oblivion final as that of fabulous Atlantis. With its end went something more than a house—something that shall be forever irrecoverable. . . .

PLATE 73

ELEGY FOR THE OLD SOUTH (NO. 3)

ONE of the techniques whereby photography may be made more responsive to the demands of the creative imagination is that known as collage. The collage method consists in selecting images from various photographic prints (or, even, other types of reproductions), cutting certain chosen portions out, and then re-combining them into a composite print, when they can be re-photographed if one wishes. By this means a hyper-realism can be achieved—since now there is present (if the collage is successful) an integration, and a dramatic contrast, of images from mutually distant points. The natural world, in effect, has been assembled anew by the imagination, and as a result, the reality of the mind can be presented as well as so-called "record" reality.

In the present collage, it is quite possible to feel, and savor, the emotional quality without intellectual explanations. However, for those who prefer them, here are a few explanations: through the great time-scarred columns of Uncle Sam Plantation, destroyed in 1940 in order to set the levee back, we see the ruins of Linwood Plantation, it, too, demolished (see Plate 40). From the broken roof of Linwood rises a nameless shadow, the departing "spirit of place" perhaps; from its door trips a neo-romantic cherub (a portion of a fine cast iron railing) mourning departed glories; through the overhanging black sky, with its ominous suggestions, flees the bird of happiness (an extremely rare iron design of which there seems to be but one example left in New Orleans). Here is the hyper-reality evocative of the death of a culture. . . .

PLATE 74

VICTORIAN FACADE

Afton Villa (1790-1849)

THROUGHOUT this book the attempt has been to present the full range of Louisiana plantation architecture up to the Civil War, including not only examples of the traditional houses, but also those which are rare, in some few cases, unique. It is to this latter category Afton Villa belongs. Stranger still, it is actually a house within a house.

The Barrow family, builders of Afton Villa, came from North Carolina in 1798. Selling all her immovable possessions Mrs. Olivia Ruffin Barrow, a widow, with six of her children—three of them grown—came to Louisiana by wagon train. Shortly after their arrival the family founded the house afterwards known as Highlands. The three grown sons became planters, and prospered. One of them, Bartholomew, made his home in a simple pioneer house of two floors and eight rooms, built about 1790 by a man named John Crocker, whose immense land holdings around St. Francisville, the Barrows acquired. In the early 1820's the house became the property of Bartholomew's son, David, who had been born in it in 1805. David married the daughter of a North Carolina tobacco plantation owner, with whom he eloped while ostensibly on his way to study at Princeton University, at the age of nineteen. By this wife David had a son, and a daughter named Mary. Mary, who became a noted belle, had, besides, a fine voice. It was her oft-requested rendering of Burns' lament "Flow Gently, Sweet Afton" which gave the later house its name. After some years David Barrow's wife died. In the late 1840's he re-married, his second wife being a beautiful Kentuckian, younger than himself, named Susan Woolfolk. She soon felt that a man of David Barrow's wealth and position deserved a better house than the simple one he still had. He gave his consent to any sort of house she wished—but on one condition: the old house, because of its associations, must be included in the new structure. So in 1849 work began, and the present house was actually built around the earlier one—the latter structure remaining almost intact and still retaining its original roof—so that it was about three feet under the new roof of the former!

David Barrow was practically ruined by the Civil War, and at his death in 1874, the house passed to the Howell family, who held it for more than thirty years. Following this, the house lay abandoned for three years, crumbling. Then it was taken over by Smith Bowman, a distant relative of David Barrow's second wife, who kept it till 1915 when Dr. Robert E. Lewis purchased it, and went to great pains and expense to restore the house and the grounds. In 1945, it found, again, new owners, Mr. and Mrs. Wallace Percy, related to the former owners of Greenwood Plantation (Plate 42), who are taking excellent care of the house and bringing the gardens to an even higher state of perfection.

In the opposite picture we see the front of the house, and an iron beflowered bench, which bcomes a sort of metallic phantom, placed here not only to help fill the otherwise blank foreground, but to provide contrast by means of its misty softness, with the sharp quality of the house.

PLATE 75

PLASTER FRETWORK

Afton Villa (1790-1849)

AFTON VILLA is said to have been modeled on a villa near Tours, France, and to have been built by a French architect, whose name does not seem to be known. If so, the French villa must have shown a markedly Victorian character, with pseudo-Gothic embellishments.

The eight rooms of the original house are now completely enveloped by the forty rooms of the new. Most of the new building is two-storied, but at its extremities are two three-storied hexagonal turrets, with battlements, and copper guns which act as rainspouts. The flamboyant woodwork of Afton Villa is truly unique for Louisiana, and all of it—groined arches, stem pillars, brackets, balusters—were hand-carved from cypress. The walls themselves are plaster over cypress timbers. Towards each side of the portico—which, incidentally, narrowly missed becoming a portcullis since the original plans called for a moat—are insert porches. The cathedral windows contain Belgian glass.

Within the entrance hall is a great hand-carved Gothic Revival staircase, which is considered by many to be equal to that of any English manor house of the period. There are also vault ribs, carved doors, spindles, and mouldings in the same neo-Gothic style. The woodwork in the rooms near the entrance hall has been painted to imitate yellow Italian marble, basalt, and other materials.

The really superb white ballroom, however—set in a wing of the house—contains none of these pseudo effects. It is beautifully executed and restored, has a fine ceiling medallion (Plate 75), and some remarkable pierced plaster-work cornices. These cornices, of course, join ceiling and walls, but so intricate is the leaf and grape cluster design used, that the open space behind them can scarcely be seen. They represent outstanding skill. Nor should we fail to mention the Dresden China door knobs of this room, whose floral designs—each different from the other—are executed in colors whose softness and delicacy are exquisite. The present owners, Mr. and Mrs. Wallace Percy, it may be added, have greatly enriched the collection of fine furniture and antiques in the house, having traced and recovered some of the original furniture.

PLATE 76
THE MAGNIFICENT SPIRAL (NO. 3)
Afton Villa (1790-1849)

AFTON VILLA's greatest glory, it might be ventured, is the spiral staircase enclosed in a square tower near the ballroom. It rises the full three floors. Whatever difference of opinion there may be about the house itself as architecture, there can be none about the staircase.

In a clear tight spiral it swirls aloft with almost unequalled grace. As we look directly upward (Plate 76), its lines are as pure as those of the inner whorls of a sea shell. It is so well executed that some experts believe it would stand alone should it happen that the rest of the house was removed. It represents a stage of craftsmanship hardly possible in our time.

It is impossible to close on Afton Villa without calling attention to its gardens, which are truly magnificent. A series of terraces has been created along the gentle ridge on which the house was built, and these lead down into the sunken gardens. Everywhere there are hundreds of azaleas, a myriad of roses, camellias, lilies, and hedges of boxwood. A half-mile meandering avenue of live oaks leads to the house sitting in the midst of its gracious gardens.

PLATE 77

A LOUISIANA RARITY

Orange Grove Plantation (1850)

LIKE Afton Villa, Orange Grove Plantation is unique in Louisiana. It is as though a giant with a wry sense of humor, addicted to kidnapping houses, had set down an English manor house with some Tudor details, in the cane fields of the Magnolia State. It was erected in 1850, by Thomas Asheton Morgan, whose family had played important parts in the Revolutionary War, and had had Morgantown, Pa., named after them. Morgan himself was of Welsh descent, his home being Philadelphia, but so enamoured did he become of Louisiana while visiting, that he settled here, and become a great sugar planter. He bought land below New Orleans, and his holdings, in time, had a river frontage of four full miles.

It is said that every brick, every piece of tile and timber for the house was brought from Philadelphia by chartered boat. The actual construction was done by slaves, but the extensive hand-carved details were shipped finished. Its only concession to local tradition was a pillared gallery encircling the main floor, which has since been ripped off the house. The main three-floored structure, which is entirely brick, has four enormous rooms with twenty-foot ceilings, and a great hall, with pointed arches and carved Gothic doors, on the first floor; above, the two other floors have six rooms each, with massive embrasures, latticed windows, and shutters which fold in three sections, like tryptichs. Looking towards the rear of the house (Plate 77) a two-storied brick wing emerges, with eight rooms which were used for the servants and the kitchens. Door knobs throughout the house were silver, there was stained glass in the windows and transoms, tile on the roof (now replaced by sheet metal) and the hall floor was of black and white marble tiles. Another non-indigenous feature was a brick basement which extended several feet above ground. Morgan, far in advance of his time, tried to solve the usual inadequate sanitary facilities characteristic of the houses of the period by having built, on each of the upper floors, a huge stone basin with a small furnace beneath. From these basins ran copper pipes into the bedrooms, which were operated by faucets so that hot water could be obtained when servants lit the furnaces. Another unusual feature of the house was two great fireplaces—whose mantels and hearths were cast in one piece of iron.

Once there was a lovely drive lined with oaks and magnolias before the house, with marble fish ponds and fountains in the gardens. These now are gone. And the house lies abandoned—all its lines solid and unyielding, its sharp gables piercing the soft air like halberds—but strangely empty, strangely unrelated to its setting, a massive and mysterious intruder, with the vines, an invading horde, climbing into its gaping windows.

PLATE 78

THE DARK LADY

The Myrtles (about 1850)

LITTLE seems known concerning the history of this house. It is said to have been built about 1850 by Judge Clark Woodruff of the Felicianas. Now owned by Mr. and Mrs. Surget Williams, it is an extremely long frame structure with two huge dormers, which actually become rooms, set between three smaller dormers. The structure is partly encircled by a broad verandah, enclosed with fine cast-iron railings and standards, and embodying a grape cluster motif. Within, there are marble mantels, excellent plaster ornamentation, silver door knobs; and some of the original wallpaper still remains. It has been kept in a condition approaching perfection by its owners.

A number of ghost stories have become associated with The Myrtles. One of these concerns an infant who, throughout the night, cries in its former death chamber. Another is that of an old French lady who wanders, sometimes at night, from room to room, lifting mosquito *baires*, and searching, evidently, for some unknown person she never finds. Plate 78 suggests the return of this unknown from the great gulf of the past; that past, which mathematicians now assure us, is co-existent with the present.

PLATE 71　TEMPLE TO A MISPLACED PAST

Uncle Sam Plantation (1843-1849)

Fagot himself seems to have retained, through the years, the original simplicity of his personal needs. Then, too, there was about him something of austerity, tempered with gentleness that showed itself in his treatment of his numerous youthful relatives, whose familiar appellation, "Uncle Sam's place," probably gave the house its name, and, as well, his slaves, for whom he provided both a church and a hospital. But to the end—his death came shortly before the outbreak of the Civil War—Samuel Fagot remained the vital spark at the heart of this huge plantation; the man through whose single life poured multiple living currents from the lives of the numerous slaves, the countless visitors, the plentiful relatives, the myriad existences of growing and moving things—the great green waves of the cane, the crystalline tide of the processed sugar, the ripening fruit of the trees, the thick flood of the Mississippi, the ships that bore the culture of France, the seeds of ideas—integrating all these things into one sentient whole; a man who never knew the dead world of numerals, of paper profits—who knew only, and always, the life of the earth, the riches of the soil; who could sense, directly and immediately, the meaning of wealth.

With Samuel Fagot's death, management of the plantation passed to Lucien Malus, husband of Félicie—one of Samuel Fagot's two daughters—under whose direction the plantation managed to weather the Reconstruction period.

Lucien and Félicie Malus, in turn, had two daughters, who married two brothers, Jules and Camile Jacobs. The Jacobs brothers, too, were energetic and succeeded in retaining some measure of prosperity at the plantation despite what was happening coincidentally elsewhere. They were, for example, the first planters in that part of Louisiana to use tractors on a large scale. Some of the same machinery they introduced, abandoned and rusty, remained on the broad verandahs of the main house during its last days. Plate 69 with its luminous gray tones, conveys something of the special melancholy of the house towards the close of its life. Notwithstanding their efforts, however, the far reaching results of the economic twilight following the Civil War, together with the later and as disastrous effects due to competition from increased foreign production of sugar, and, also, disease of the cane itself, could not, finally, be evaded.

PLATE 72   TRANSPLANTED FRANCE

Uncle Sam Plantation (1843-1849)

About 1915, Jules Jacobs sold the plantation to a New Orleans commission merchant—and the great house then had seen its final days of human occupancy—there being no one who could afford keeping it in proper condition.

Meanwhile, the river, silent and implacable, had been creeping ever closer, drawing its coils tighter about the house, undermining the upstream side of the bend enclosing the plantation. Successive levee set-backs had to take place. With them went the fine lawns, the wharves, the oak alleys. At length, in the spring of 1940, the ultimate blow was struck. The U. S. Engineers, in charge of all levee construction and protection along the Mississippi River, determined that still another set-back must be made, if a levee failure was to be avoided. And so, demolition of Uncle Sam, of all its buildings, was commenced. At the time of its destruction, it was probably the most complete plantation group left in the entire South. Ironically enough, on March 12 of that year, the U. S. Engineer Office in New Orleans received the following telegram from the Director of the National Park Service in Washington:

> Have learned of the impending demolition of the Uncle Sam Plantation near Convent, Louisiana. Stop. Can demolition be deferred short time pending investigation by National Park Service to determine possibilities for status as a national monument or historic site?

It was then too late. The house was three quarters gone—its massive walls, with their irreplaceable materials and workmanship, smashed and torn into heaps of rubble. Thus, on a bitter concluding note, ends the history of Uncle Sam—lost in the slow sullen waters of the Mississippi, its site engulfed in oblivion final as that of fabulous Atlantis. With its end went something more than a house—something that shall be forever irrecoverable. . . .

PLATE 73

ELEGY FOR THE OLD SOUTH (NO. 3)

ONE of the techniques whereby photography may be made more responsive to the demands of the creative imagination is that known as collage. The collage method consists in selecting images from various photographic prints (or, even, other types of reproductions), cutting certain chosen portions out, and then re-combining them into a composite print, when they can be re-photographed if one wishes. By this means a hyper-realism can be achieved—since now there is present (if the collage is successful) an integration, and a dramatic contrast, of images from mutually distant points. The natural world, in effect, has been assembled anew by the imagination, and as a result, the reality of the mind can be presented as well as so-called "record" reality.

In the present collage, it is quite possible to feel, and savor, the emotional quality without intellectual explanations. However, for those who prefer them, here are a few explanations: through the great time-scarred columns of Uncle Sam Plantation, destroyed in 1940 in order to set the levee back, we see the ruins of Linwood Plantation, it, too, demolished (see Plate 40). From the broken roof of Linwood rises a nameless shadow, the departing "spirit of place" perhaps; from its door trips a neo-romantic cherub (a portion of a fine cast iron railing) mourning departed glories; through the overhanging black sky, with its ominous suggestions, flees the bird of happiness (an extremely rare iron design of which there seems to be but one example left in New Orleans). Here is the hyper-reality evocative of the death of a culture. . . .

PLATE 74

VICTORIAN FACADE

Afton Villa (1790-1849)

THROUGHOUT this book the attempt has been to present the full range of Louisiana plantation architecture up to the Civil War, including not only examples of the traditional houses, but also those which are rare, in some few cases, unique. It is to this latter category Afton Villa belongs. Stranger still, it is actually a house within a house.

The Barrow family, builders of Afton Villa, came from North Carolina in 1798. Selling all her immovable possessions Mrs. Olivia Ruffin Barrow, a widow, with six of her children—three of them grown—came to Louisiana by wagon train. Shortly after their arrival the family founded the house afterwards known as Highlands. The three grown sons became planters, and prospered. One of them, Bartholomew, made his home in a simple pioneer house of two floors and eight rooms, built about 1790 by a man named John Crocker, whose immense land holdings around St. Francisville, the Barrows acquired. In the early 1820's the house became the property of Bartholomew's son, David, who had been born in it in 1805. David married the daughter of a North Carolina tobacco plantation owner, with whom he eloped while ostensibly on his way to study at Princeton University, at the age of nineteen. By this wife David had a son, and a daughter named Mary. Mary, who became a noted belle, had, besides, a fine voice. It was her oft-requested rendering of Burns' lament "Flow Gently, Sweet Afton" which gave the later house its name. After some years David Barrow's wife died. In the late 1840's he re-married, his second wife being a beautiful Kentuckian, younger than himself, named Susan Woolfolk. She soon felt that a man of David Barrow's wealth and position deserved a better house than the simple one he still had. He gave his consent to any sort of house she wished—but on one condition: the old house, because of its associations, must be included in the new structure. So in 1849 work began, and the present house was actually built around the earlier one—the latter structure remaining almost intact and still retaining its original roof—so that it was about three feet under the new roof of the former!

David Barrow was practically ruined by the Civil War, and at his death in 1874, the house passed to the Howell family, who held it for more than thirty years. Following this, the house lay abandoned for three years, crumbling. Then it was taken over by Smith Bowman, a distant relative of David Barrow's second wife, who kept it till 1915 when Dr. Robert E. Lewis purchased it, and went to great pains and expense to restore the house and the grounds. In 1945, it found, again, new owners, Mr. and Mrs. Wallace Percy, related to the former owners of Greenwood Plantation (Plate 42), who are taking excellent care of the house and bringing the gardens to an even higher state of perfection.

In the opposite picture we see the front of the house, and an iron beflowered bench, which bcomes a sort of metallic phantom, placed here not only to help fill the otherwise blank foreground, but to provide contrast by means of its misty softness, with the sharp quality of the house.

PLATE 75

PLASTER FRETWORK

Afton Villa (1790-1849)

AFTON VILLA is said to have been modeled on a villa near Tours, France, and to have been built by a French architect, whose name does not seem to be known. If so, the French villa must have shown a markedly Victorian character, with pseudo-Gothic embellishments.

The eight rooms of the original house are now completely enveloped by the forty rooms of the new. Most of the new building is two-storied, but at its extremities are two three-storied hexagonal turrets, with battlements, and copper guns which act as rainspouts. The flamboyant woodwork of Afton Villa is truly unique for Louisiana, and all of it—groined arches, stem pillars, brackets, balusters—were hand-carved from cypress. The walls themselves are plaster over cypress timbers. Towards each side of the portico—which, incidentally, narrowly missed becoming a portcullis since the original plans called for a moat—are insert porches. The cathedral windows contain Belgian glass.

Within the entrance hall is a great hand-carved Gothic Revival staircase, which is considered by many to be equal to that of any English manor house of the period. There are also vault ribs, carved doors, spincles, and mouldings in the same neo-Gothic style. The woodwork in the rooms near the entrance hall has been painted to imitate yellow Italian marble, basalt, and other materials.

The really superb white ballroom, however—set in a wing of the house—contains none of these pseudo effects. It is beautifully executed and restored, has a fine ceiling medallion (Plate 75), and some remarkable pierced plaster-work cornices. These cornices, of course, join ceiling and walls, but so intricate is the leaf and grape cluster design used, that the open space behind them can scarcely be seen. They represent outstanding skill. Nor should we fail to mention the Dresden China door knobs of this room, whose floral designs—each different from the other—are executed in colors whose softness and delicacy are exquisite. The present owners, Mr. and Mrs. Wallace Percy, it may be added, have greatly enriched the collection of fine furniture and antiques in the house, having traced and recovered some of the original furniture.

PLATE 76

THE MAGNIFICENT SPIRAL (NO. 3)

Afton Villa (1790-1849)

AFTON VILLA's greatest glory, it might be ventured, is the spiral staircase enclosed in a square tower near the ballroom. It rises the full three floors. Whatever difference of opinion there may be about the house itself as architecture, there can be none about the staircase.

In a clear tight spiral it swirls aloft with almost unequalled grace. As we look directly upward (Plate 76), its lines are as pure as those of the inner whorls of a sea shell. It is so well executed that some experts believe it would stand alone should it happen that the rest of the house was removed. It represents a stage of craftsmanship hardly possible in our time.

It is impossible to close on Afton Villa without calling attention to its gardens, which are truly magnificent. A series of terraces has been created along the gentle ridge on which the house was built, and these lead down into the sunken gardens. Everywhere there are hundreds of azaleas, a myriad of roses, camellias, lilies, and hedges of boxwood. A half-mile meandering avenue of live oaks leads to the house sitting in the midst of its gracious gardens.

PLATE 77

A LOUISIANA RARITY

Orange Grove Plantation (1850)

LIKE Afton Villa, Orange Grove Plantation is unique in Louisiana. It is as though a giant with a wry sense of humor, addicted to kidnapping houses, had set down an English manor house with some Tudor details, in the cane fields of the Magnolia State. It was erected in 1850, by Thomas Asheton Morgan, whose family had played important parts in the Revolutionary War, and had had Morgantown, Pa., named after them. Morgan himself was of Welsh descent, his home being Philadelphia, but so enamoured did he become of Louisiana while visiting, that he settled here, and become a great sugar planter. He bought land below New Orleans, and his holdings, in time, had a river frontage of four full miles.

It is said that every brick, every piece of tile and timber for the house was brought from Philadelphia by chartered boat. The actual construction was done by slaves, but the extensive hand-carved details were shipped finished. Its only concession to local tradition was a pillared gallery encircling the main floor, which has since been ripped off the house. The main three-floored structure, which is entirely brick, has four enormous rooms with twenty-foot ceilings, and a great hall, with pointed arches and carved Gothic doors, on the first floor; above, the two other floors have six rooms each, with massive embrasures, latticed windows, and shutters which fold in three sections, like tryptichs. Looking towards the rear of the house (Plate 77) a two-storied brick wing emerges, with eight rooms which were used for the servants and the kitchens. Door knobs throughout the house were silver, there was stained glass in the windows and transoms, tile on the roof (now replaced by sheet metal) and the hall floor was of black and white marble tiles. Another non-indigenous feature was a brick basement which extended several feet above ground. Morgan, far in advance of his time, tried to solve the usual inadequate sanitary facilities characteristic of the houses of the period by having built, on each of the upper floors, a huge stone basin with a small furnace beneath. From these basins ran copper pipes into the bedrooms, which were operated by faucets so that hot water could be obtained when servants lit the furnaces. Another unusual feature of the house was two great fireplaces—whose mantels and hearths were cast in one piece of iron.

Once there was a lovely drive lined with oaks and magnolias before the house, with marble fish ponds and fountains in the gardens. These now are gone. And the house lies abandoned—all its lines solid and unyielding, its sharp gables piercing the soft air like halberds—but strangely empty, strangely unrelated to its setting, a massive and mysterious intruder, with the vines, an invading horde, climbing into its gaping windows.

PLATE 78

THE DARK LADY

The Myrtles (about 1850)

LITTLE seems known concerning the history of this house. It is said to have been built about 1850 by Judge Clark Woodruff of the Felicianas. Now owned by Mr. and Mrs. Surget Williams, it is an extremely long frame structure with two huge dormers, which actually become rooms, set between three smaller dormers. The structure is partly encircled by a broad verandah, enclosed with fine cast-iron railings and standards, and embodying a grape cluster motif. Within, there are marble mantels, excellent plaster ornamentation, silver door knobs; and some of the original wallpaper still remains. It has been kept in a condition approaching perfection by its owners.

A number of ghost stories have become associated with The Myrtles. One of these concerns an infant who, throughout the night, cries in its former death chamber. Another is that of an old French lady who wanders, sometimes at night, from room to room, lifting mosquito *baires*, and searching, evidently, for some unknown person she never finds. Plate 78 suggests the return of this unknown from the great gulf of the past; that past, which mathematicians now assure us, is co-existent with the present.

PLATE 87

GRANDEUR AND DECAY (NO. 5)

Belle Grove Plantation (1856?-1857)

ALL the previous pictures of Belle Grove were made in the years 1939 and 1940. In late 1945 Belle Grove was re-visited. We are witnesses now to how much further the destruction of this great house has progressed within this comparatively short intervening period. Before us is the same rear wall and gallery we saw in Plate 86, but seen from an opposite diagonal. Aloft, huge cavernous openings yawn where further portions of the walls have collapsed.

An effort was made to save Belle Grove in 1940. Overwhelmed by the stricken beauty of the house, as they saw it in the pages of the November 1939 issue of *House and Garden*, two brothers, John and William Wickes of Saginaw, Michigan, bought Belle Grove early in 1940, hoping to be able to raise enough money to restore it to its former glory. Costs of restoration, it was found, might very probably be well over a million dollars; in addition, it was doubtful whether some of Belle Grove's materials could ever be replaced—the great cypress beams, for instance; or whether all the craftsmanship could be duplicated—the huge hand-carved capitals, the incomparable spiral staircase (now collapsed), the intricately molded plaster work. Finally, one more factor ominously loomed—the river. Built near the extremity of a great bend in the Mississippi, Belle Grove had become the hapless target of the southwestward eating of the river. Already, most of the grove of oaks from which the house partly takes its name, was gone.

Whether it was inability to raise sufficient funds, or because of the constantly growing threat of the river, the plans, apparently, fell through. Then, once more, in 1945, new owners appeared —Mr. and Mrs. F. J. Nehrbass of Lafayette, La.—only to find themselves unable to cut the inexorable knot of circumstance; only to be forced to stand helplessly and despairingly by while time and the water conspired to bring about the ultimate ruin of the house. And so Belle Grove remains, a doomed and lonely outpost, lost in time, of a pattern of living whose scale can no longer be made to fit into ours.

Note: Latest research—by Mr. Sam Wilson—has proved that the architect for Belle Grove was not the Galliers, as previously supposed, but Henry Howard, the designer of another great Louisiana plantation house, Nottaway, as well as of several outstanding mansions in New Orleans.

PLATE 88

THE ENSHADOWED PILLARS (NO. 1)

Belle Grove Plantation (1856?-1857)

WE are given here the complete side elevation of Belle Grove—that side which is to the right, or upstream, as we face the front of the house. We can now obtain a full view of the verandah seen diagonally to the left of Plate 86. This particular aspect of the house comes as close to giving us the original feeling of the huge structure as any which it is now possible to obtain.

It is interesting to note the arrangement of the shutters. There were four shutters to each great window; each of these could be operated separately; and each, in turn, could be folded back on itself; being divided, also, into a solid portion, and a louvered portion. Note, too, the scale of the massive foundation arches. The fluted columns, of course, were plastered brick and their enormous six-foot capitals, amazingly enough, were of cypress wood, applied in four sections around the brick cores of the columns, and gilded. Some of these capitals have withstood weathering even better than the pillars which bear them.

PLATE 89

THE ENSHADOWED PILLARS (NO. 3)

Belle Grove Plantation (1856?-1857)

IN close-up, a portion of the huge dexter gallery seen fully in Plate 88, appears here. Distantly, one of the columns of the front portico is visible. The dramatic and powerful alternations of light and dark on the mighty pillar give us a sense of the true grandeur of Belle Grove. Not only is the tremendous soaring of the column accentuated, but it can be observed that in the beautiful modulation of light and dark towards the upper right, a strange and suspended phantasm seems to appear; aiding further the element of architectural interpretation, rather than that of simple recording. . . .

Beneath its cloak of commonplace, the essentially strange process whereby solid things, such as buildings, revert to shadow; and then, once more, appear again under the chemistry of time and the mind, holds a fascination intimately allied to the magic of the plantation houses—a magic which we feel so strongly here.

PLATE 90

THE HEAD IN THE CEILING

Belle Grove Plantation (1856?-1857)

WITHIN Belle Grove, remnants of the exquisite delicacy of the interior ornamentation still linger. Finely proportioned Corinthian columns are well spaced in the huge halls and near the entrance to the lower turret room; and a large number of pilasters are used. Surprisingly enough, these columns and their capitals, are carved wood; but much excellent plaster work remains on the ceilings and dentilled cornices. As has been previously mentioned, the original spiral staircase of Belle Grove—as fine, possibly, as that which formerly existed in the old St. Louis Hotel in New Orleans—collapsed some years ago. It is no longer possible to get to the upper floors. Everywhere are places where the flooring has fallen through, or has been deliberately ripped up by vandals, searching for materials.

But it was the failure of the roof some years since which was the immediate factor spelling Belle Grove's doom. As we enter one of the vast ruined drawing rooms of the main floor and look up at the ceiling, we see how the rain has been falling through all the great floors, cracking, discoloring, and loosening all the fine plaster and woodwork (Plate 90). And we see, too, the monstrous and beast-like head made by a broken plaster area in this ceiling, with its snout towards the lower left of the picture. Fancy, perhaps; but the images of our fancy often have a subtle and living relationship with that secret and inner world which is created by conceiving forms as symbols; by conceiving architecture as, fundamentally, an extension of the human mind. . . .

The walls of other deserted rooms are scabrous with damp, and in them, new, and disquieting colors have appeared; colors as though from the death of a living thing. . . .

An important component in the delicacy conveyed by the house despite its size, in its mysterious appeal to the imagination, is the subtle way colors were used to integrate the forms, and to give warmth to the walls. The white woodwork was under-painted with a base of lavender-rose, thus effectively killing any effect of coldness. The plaster was painted first blue, then pink, with a final wash of lavender. On the columns and exterior walls the blue was omitted. There were some even more subtle variations on various other surfaces. And thus, a perfection of color was achieved which not only tied the various elements of the house together, but gave it the air of a roseate gem, flushed with life.

PLATE 91

NEO-ROMANTIC ELEGY

Belle Grove Plantation (1856?-1857)

AGAINST one of the tremendous broken walls of Belle Grove two images were made on one negative of the same Greek plaster head, creating a poem to the great structure where Grecian purity and severity re-appeared in so strange a guise; where classic grandeur has a haunting quality most non-classic and romantic. The concept of the head which swallows itself is a symbol of the complex way by which plantation culture devoured itself from within. . . .

PLATE 92

TRAGIC STILL-LIFE

Belle Grove Plantation (1856?-1857)

USING fragments of the broken capitals and the fallen florets of Belle Grove, together with a wisp of the moss which obscures the air about the house, this symbolic and tragic still-life was arranged on top of a dismantled door. Here, in these shattered fragments, and the shred of moss which is like the ominous cloth of dismay, is the ultimate and evocative residue of plantation glory.

Meanwhile, Belle Grove waits, horribly isolate now; its last hopes of restoration gone, while the river creeps inexorably closer. Steeped in unutterable loneliness and ruin, it waits; mouldering amid its tremendous oaks, draped in their great grey mourning gowns of moss—an appropriate end to a culture whose decay was as rapid as its rise. . . .

PLATE 93

THE OAK ARCH

Woodlawn Plantation (1835-1839)

WEST of the Mississippi, in the Lafourche country—one of the strangest, and most highly individualized sections of Louisiana—there stood, till recently, the ruins of Woodlawn Plantation; ruins which spoke a subtly appropriate language in a land the banks of whose lonely moss-gloomed bayous are enwrithed by cypress roots; pitted by the burrows of fiddler crabs and crayfish; upon whose languorous slow-flowing streams the willows set their water-loving garlands, the oaks, their funereal streamers of moss; while above, in great heavy masses of foliage and monster-like limbs, night seems to find its abode even in the midst of day—and a kind of living darkness appears to grow. . . . So dense are these oak growths, so enormous because of their absorption of light, that the very water flowing below—so secretively, so soundlessly—seems thickened and tinged with dissolved shadow. . . .

As we approached the ruins in 1941, they became framed in a gigantic oak arch whose gray uneasy trailers of moss appeared as though the vestments of the tree had turned to rags—torn by a wind out of time. . . . And then, as immediate contrast, we noted that to the left of the ruins a great pine, charged by the sun, sent up its pattern of needles, like static discharges—and how the light, coming from beyond it, bathed it in a mysterious and electronic glow—the strange secret fire that imbues and animates all living things. . . .

It was in this setting that William W. Pugh, still quite young, yet possessed by one knows not what vision of splendor decided to build his house. Some years earlier, in 1818, his father had sold all his possessions in North Carolina—and with him, at the age of nine, he had made the long journey to the kingdom of the moss and the cypress. His kinfolk being among the very first American settlers in this region, something in it must have spoken to the youthful William in that remote language which only our nerves—and not our words—know; only the things that relate us to the slow green-growing tree; the slow dark-flowing water. And here, in 1839, the house was completed. . . .

Despite the use of slave labor, the sum of $70,000, together with four years of work, were required for its erection. The four huge plastered brick Ionic pillars were actually given stone capitals—something unique in the plantation architecture of Louisiana; the two temple-like wings, of exquisite proportions, extended backwards, so that small enclosed courts were formed between them and the main body of the house. In these courts visitors could sit, enjoy the art of conversation, and the cool of the evening, fine coffee served in porcelain from France, pungent cigars that only the perique tobacco of Louisiana made possible. . . . Woodlawn incorporated other refinements, too. It is said to have had the first installation of gas in any of the Louisiana plantation houses. Also, it had a bathroom with a marble tub—a very advanced feature for its time.

William W. Pugh became enormously wealthy, his family extending its holdings throughout the Lafourche country; constructing, among other things, another great house, Madewood (Plate 66). From 1854 to 1858 he was speaker in the Louisiana House of Representatives, and served with distinction throughout the Civil War. He escaped from the memorable Last Island

PLATE 94   ELEGY FOR AN OLD HOUSE
Woodlawn Plantation (1855-1859)

hurricane which thundered out of the Gulf of Mexico on August 10, 1856—sweeping the most fashionable and luxurious southern summer hotel of that era, and most of its guests, into the sea—and it was not till 1906, at the age of ninety-five, that he died, leaving behind him fifteen children, and hosts of grandchildren. Leaving behind him, too, the waning of his family. . . . In 1910 Woodlawn was sold, and in July, 1941, the heir of all its grandeur was one lone Negro caretaker—powerless to allay the acid of time. At that date, in the immense chambers of one of its wings, hay for farm animals was being stored, and the drip of this hay from the windows was repeated, in a more ominous key, by the grey ghostly rain of the moss that fell from the great oak overhanging the side of the house (see Plate 94).

Age had mellowed the tints of Woodlawn to a lovely fusion—salmon pink in the plastered surfaces of the wings and pillars, soft greenish-blue in the tall blinds, ghostly white, streaked with dark, over the wooden portions of the entablature. Seen on a stage properly set for this neo-romantic drama of glory and decay—in an ethereal glowing sunset light (the light in which these pictures were made)—there seeped from Woodlawn a feeling of poignant and special melancholy; a melancholy compounded of factors other than those immediately meeting the eye—for in this special light there emerged from it something more than the spectacle of ruin; something due to a sense of its complete isolation in time; something utterly tragic because of our realization that here a certain pattern of life had found a form to which it was fitted with the most exquisite precision—and that, from this form, life had now almost wholly receded. . . . And this light, too, silent, remote and infinitely searching, clinging to the house in a film thinner and lighter than any bubble; enclosing with magic nostalgia this solid dream from out the past; this light that discovered, nevertheless, each grain and hollow in the texture of the walls— revealed the features of the house as a complex countenance whose inhuman gaze made known to us, in a timeless instant of terrible joy, the shadow that besets us, the flame that dwells in all our tissues, the reality of that which we usually dismiss as unreal. . . . Soft and sinister as the clinging shadows of the leaves on the walls; sharp as the soundless explosions of light about the looming figures that, at times, seemed to congeal from the hollow darkness of the upper rooms, was the strange feeling this place aroused—the feeling of being torn out of our proper place in time and space, and to have found again, somehow, a world long flown down the stream of the years, a world far from our unceasing modern strife. Time is a dream, said one of the greatest of poets, and it was here, at Woodlawn, that we realized this to the full; here that we sensed that contemporary mathematical theories as to the nature of time—time as a fourth dimension through which one might be able to move under certain circumstances; of the past, present and future as being equally co-existent—might be no more fantastic, no more strange, than this object which confronted us; this feeling which seized us and whirled us away on a dark temporal stream; this structure whose very form was determined by the pattern made by the desires and fears of those long dead. . . .

PLATE 95 FAREWELL TO THE PAST (No. 5)

Woodlawn Plantation (1835-1839)

And with this realization there arose the conviction that, within these walls of Woodlawn, the wraiths out of a past which only our incompletely developed senses prevented from being wholly visible, were on the verge of becoming tangible, despite all barriers. . . . Yet not ever, wholly . . . Shut within the limitations of our sensory organization, desperate, we could go back only to the disquieting knowledge that here time, under whose shadow we live, became no longer a mere word, but an awful engine which, under the acceleration of Louisiana heat and dampness, had beaten the very pillars into softened and slowly crumbling forms, forms imperceptibly becoming impalpable; forms which would revert, finally, to shadows only, living a strange life in other minds to come, while our own reached backward; and how forlornly, to a time, and a life, whose beauty and gentleness are now no more, and can never be again. . . .

And, returning again to the front of the house, we steeped ourselves once more in the mournful and majestic beauty of the columns (Plate 95); sensing, rather than seeing, the black melancholy figure which grew mysteriously from the fluted luminance of a distant pillar. . . .

PLATE 96

THE APPARITION

Woodlawn Plantation (1835-1839)

IT should be stressed, since so many still do not seem to realize it, that the camera can be responsive to the quality of an individual imagination in the same sense, though, of course, not by means of the same technique as the painter's brush. It can be an instrumentation for producing a poetic concentration of reality, just as painting can be.

An example of this use of the camera is Plate 96, where a synthesis of reality has been produced which effectively projects the magic and enigma of old houses. This is expressed by the moss now dripping from within the house, the hay falling through the cavernous walls, the mysterious and beautiful architectural dislocation (suggesting dislocation in time), the movement of the pillars back and forth in space, the shadow figure which itself casts a shadow.

The shadow figure, it might be added, conveys a feeling of being a time phantasm, an image which crystallizes our haunting sense of time existing here in the form of another dimension; of these sombre and brooding walls being, somehow, a living extension out of the past. . . .

PLATE 97

THE MOSS WEEPS

Woodlawn Plantation (1835-1839)

WHEN, toward the end of 1946, we returned, after a lapse of some years, years which seemed far longer than they were, to Woodlawn, it was to discover a disquieting and truly tragic sight. It was to behold the final episode in the drama of Woodlawn. . . .

Its great capitals littered the ground, scattered as though by a giant. The entire central portion of the house was demolished, the magnificent columns toppled; only portions of the wings remained. While towards the rear, the dark and deathly forest pressed closer. . . .

PLATE 98

ELEGY FOR THE OLD SOUTH (NO. 6)

Woodlawn Plantation (1835-1859)

LOOKING with the eye of the mind, which, driven by memory and desire, re-combines the elements of the natural world, we see the inner essence of the tragedy of Woodlawn.

One fallen capital, the exquisite pattern of whose necking repeats the anthemion motif of that of the Erechtheum, opens—and discloses to us the last gaunt and dismembered remains of Woodlawn. The shadows seem ominously active. With a sense of chill foreboding we see that the dark forest has come closer still; there is an ambiguous thronging of leaves and tendrils over the roofs and walls. The house seems to be receding from us, as though it were moving back into the shadows of the past; as though, as we watch, it is becoming hidden from us by the veils of untold years. . . . And the moss falls, in a ghastly rain of intolerable grieving. . . .

PLATE 99

THE LAUGHTER OF RUIN

Woodlawn Plantation (1835-1839)

AND Ruin opened its iron mouth, and laughed, its hideous laughter clanging down the corridors of our stricken heart. Cruel and insatiable, its great metal face rose before our eyes, avid and rident over the altar of so much dead beauty; filled with a sense of its ineluctable and ever-growing power . . . It is the face that hangs over all our world. . . .

Thus, in a blaze of bitter grandeur ends the overshadowed and tragic history of Woodlawn. . . .

Note: The iron face springs integrally from plantation house material. It is, actually, a carefully selected portion of a fallen fragment of one of Windsor Plantation's great fallen capitals.

PLATE 100
THE FINAL BELL

MOST Louisiana plantations possessed a bell, used for calling the slaves to their labors in the fields. Such a bell can be seen now, hanging silent, on its uncertain perch, against a still and twilit sky.

Afar, tiny clouds, curiously shaped and infinitely remote, are like tender and troubled intimations, hovering on the verge of the inexpressible—of a life, and a world, engulfed forever by the mystery of time. . . .

While the bell stays soundless; with an utter and overwhelming finality; as though it has just tolled the death of plantation culture, and now must remain, its tongue forever still—in the silent and now darkening air. . . .

ACKNOWLEDGMENTS

I take great pleasure in acknowledging my indebtedness to:

Mrs. Durel Black
Mr. and Mrs. Frank N. Boatner
Miss Josie Cerf
Mrs. Ida Churchill
Dr. George B. Crozat
Miss Marguerite Fortier
Mrs. Matilda Gray
Prof. Talbot Hamlin
Mr. Richard Hammer
Dr. George L. Hardin
Mrs. Jefferson D. Hardin, Jr.
Mr. Philip Harsham
Mrs. Cammie Garrett Henry
Mr. Wilmer Hinrichs
Dr. and Mrs. E. G. Kohlsdorf
Mr. Arthur La Salle
Mrs. Renée Charles La Salle
Miss Rosalie L. Matthews
Mrs. Walter C. Parlange
Prof. Buford L. Pickens
Miss Marguerite D. Renshaw
Mrs. C. J. Rogers
Mr. Curtiss Schroeder
Dr. Herman de Bachellé Seebold
Mrs. John Smyth
Mr. I. H. Stauffer
Mr. and Mrs. Edgar B. Stern
Mrs. Andrew Stewart
Dr. Garland Taylor
Mrs. Mildred Taylor
Mr. Sam Wilson, Jr.

and, finally, but not least, to: Mr. William B. Wisdom
—all of whom, in various ways, were greatly helpful in making this book possible.

EPILOGUE

SUCH are some of the histories of Louisiana's houses, too long to tell here in complete detail; too tragic for words alone to capture, since it has been expressed so well, so completely in great crumbling masses of wood and brick and stone; in walls cracked by the resistless and feverish searchings of plant roots; in stains from the hot caresses of the rain; the melancholia of great oaks, draped in their mourning gowns of grey moss; the smell of the magnolia whose scent is nearly tangible, summoning up a richness that seems, at times, to cling to the walls like a materialized memory; the violence of decay that produces in these surfaces colors as though from a sinister fairyland—in all these things the grandeur and decay of plantation culture is written in a language wholly integral with the things it describes. . . .

And these, but a few of the little-known, and tragic, chronicles of the shadow, which is time; and of the light, which is life—tales set in a land where the Mississippi, immense and heavy, shoulders the levees; a land where the earth melts imperceptibly into river and marsh; where moss reigns over unmoving and menacing water; where time, light, and the river have formed an intricate and fateful web whose conformations have never found a duplicate elsewhere. . . .

Herein, too, is conveyed some part of the strange and difficult beauty of Louisiana, for which we, who have loved her, can only cry: Louisiana, ruin-haunted land; land of the writhing, ever-coiling bayous, whose passages are lined with the grey dolorous membranes of moss; land of the magnolia whose wild sweetness becomes almost visible because of its heavy burden of remembrance; land of broken white columns struggling amid fierce green hordes of foliage; land of shadow-haunted and shadow-silent waters, mirroring a brooding that knows no bounds—a feeling of being lost forever in the savage and magical wilderness of time, where the past and the present have become one, and are forever and inextricably mingled! Louisiana: to thy moist teeming earth; to thy flat dark mirrors overhung with the grey clouds of moss, and the green clouds of willows; to thy lush vestments of sugar cane and rice; to thy great sails of banana trees; to thy palms, which are quivering fountains of light; to thy heavily scented and moon-amorous flowers; to thy iron growths of balconies and cemetery ornamentation; to thy simple, naïve, and earth-loving buildings of brick and plaster; to thee, whose very name is music, do our hearts turn, Louisiana!

TECHNICAL APPENDIX

A number of the negatives for this book were made in 1938 and 1939 (these negatives are identified by an "X" after the plate number); the camera used was a 9x12 cm. Karl Zeiss Nixe camera, which carried a Zeiss 6.3 Tessar lens. But the majority of the negatives were made in late 1946 and in 1947, and for these the camera was a 4x5" Korona Wood View Camera, fitted with a 4.5 Zeiss Tessar lens, of 13.5 cm. focal length.

The negative material, in all cases, was Ansco Isopan sheet film, developed in Kodak D-76 for varying times, with agitation. In most cases, care was taken to get as much shadow detail as possible.

Negatives were printed on #3 and #4 Kodabromide paper, glossy, developed in D-72 (Dektol). All prints were "controlled" (or "shaded") to retain shadow detail while printing through highlights. Enlarger was an old-model 5x7" Elwood, using a 150-watt bulb.

Negative exposures were as follows:

Plate 1: Double exposure. Exp. A: House and water: .16 1/10" with K2 Filter.
Exp. B: Figure and tree: .18 1/10" with K2 Filter. Sun bright on both exposures.
Plate 2(x): .22 1/10" with K2 Filter. Sun bright.
Plate 3: .16 1/10" no filter. Sun medium, and low.
Plate 4: .22 1/5" with K2 Filter. Sun bright.
Plate 5: .22 1/5" with K2 Filter. Sun bright.
Plate 6(x): .16 1/10" with K2 Filter. Sun bright.
Plate 7: .16 1/5" K1 Filter. Sun low, but bright.
Plate 8: .16 1/5" no filter. Partly overcast.
Plate 9: .16 1/5" with K2 Filter. Sun medium.
Plate 10: .16 1/10" with K2 Filter. Bright sun.
Plate 11(x): .22 1/5" with K2 Filter. Bright sun.
Plate 12(x): .22 1/5" with K2 Filter. Sun low, but bright.
Plate 13(x): .16 1/5" with K2 Filter. Sun bright.
Plate 14: .16 1/5" with K2 Filter. Sun bright.
Plate 15: .16 1/5" with G Filter. Sun bright.
Plate 16: Composite picture made by introducing two somewhat underexposed negatives into enlarger at the same time. Negative exposures were made with indirect daylight only. The first negative was of the mirror; the second, of an oil painting.
Plate 17: .16 1/10" no filter. Almost complete overcast.
Plate 18: Double exposure. Exp. A: View of house: .22 1/10" with K2 Filter.
Exp. B: of old and badly faded photograph, using reflected daylight as light source: .22 1/5" with K2 Filter (photo had yellowed).
Plate 19: .16 1/10" with K2 Filter. Sun bright.
Plate 20: .16 1/5" with K2 Filter. Sun bright, but indirect light only.
Plate 21: 12.5 1/2" no filter. Completely overcast.
Plate 22: .22 1/10" with K2 Filter. Sun bright.
Plate 23(x): .16 1/5" with K2 Filter. Sun bright, but partly indirect.
Plate 24: .16 1/2" with K2 Filter. Sun bright, but large shadow areas.
Plate 25: .18 1/5" with K2 Filter. Sun bright.
Plate 26: .22 1/2" with K2 Filter. Sun bright, but most parts of picture area were black.
Plate 27: .16 1/5" with K2 Filter. Sun bright.
Plate 28: .16 1/2" with K2 Filter. No reflectors, and no flash bulbs.
Plate 29: .16 1/2" with K2 Filter. Sun bright, but mostly indirect light.
Plate 30: .16 1/5" with K2 Filter. Sun bright.
Plate 31: .16 1/5" with K2 Filter. Sun medium.
Plate 32: .16 1/5" with K2 Filter. Sun bright, but getting low.
Plate 33: Double exposure. Exp. A: Close-up of house: .16 1/10" with G Filter.
Exp. B: Close-up of palmetto fronds: .16 1/10" with K2 Filter.
Plate 34: .16 1/10" with K2 Filter. Bright sun.
Plate 35: .22 1/10" with K2 Filter. Bright sun.
Plate 36: .22 1/10" with K2 Filter. Bright sun.
Plate 37: .16 1/5" with K2 Filter. Bright sun, but heavy shadows.
Plate 38: .16 1/5" with K2 Filter. Bright sun.
Plate 39: .16 3". Indirect daylight only.
Plate 40(x): .22 1/10" with K2 Filter. Bright sun.
Plate 41: .22 1/10" with K2 Filter. Bright sun.
Plate 42: .22 1/10" with K2 Filter. Bright sun.
Plate 43: .22 1/5" with K2 Filter. Sun bright, but getting low.
Plate 44: .22 1/5" with K1 Filter. Sun bright. Photo gives effect of collage, but it is direct shot.
Plate 45: .16 1/5" with K2 Filter. Sun bright, but mostly indirect.
Plate 46: .16 1/5" with K2 Filter. Sun bright.
Plate 47: .16 1/5", no filter. Almost completely overcast.
Plate 48: .16 1/5" with K2 Filter. Sun medium.
Plate 49: .16 1/5", no filter. Almost completely overcast.
Plate 50: .16 1/5" with K2 Filter. Sun bright.
Plate 51: .18 1/5", no filter. Sun bright, but mostly indirect.
Plate 52: .16 1/5" with K2 Filter. Sun medium.
Plate 53(x): .18 1/5", no filter. Sun bright, but mostly indirect.
Plate 54(x): .16 1/5" with K2 Filter. Bright sun.

Plate 55(x): .16 1/5" with K1 Filter. Sun bright, but low.
Plate 56: .22 1/10" with K2 Filter. Sun bright.
Plate 57: .22 1/5" with K2 Filter. Sun bright.
Plate 58(x): .12.5 1/5" with K2 Filter. Bright sun outside, no supplementary interior light.
Plate 59(x): .16 3", no filter. Indirect daylight only.
Plate 60: .16 1/5" with K1 Filter. Sun weak.
Plate 61: Double exposure. Exp. A: Beauregard House, New Orleans: .16 1/10" with K2 Filter.
Exp. B: Grove at Ashland Plantation: .16 1/2" with K2 Filter.
Plate 62(x): .18 1/10" with K2 Filter. Sun bright.
Plate 63: .18 1/10" with K2 Filter. Sun bright.
Plate 64: .16 1/5" with K2 Filter. Sun bright, but low.
Plate 65: .16 1/2" with K2 Filter. Sun medium.
Plate 66: .16 1/5" with K2 Filter. Sun bright.
Plate 67: Double exposure. Exp. A: Front view of house: .16 1/2" with A Filter.
Exp. B: close-up of silver emblem: .16 3", no filter, and using two #1 photofloods as illumination.
Plate 68: Double exposure. Two exposures, moving camera slightly, each exposure at .16 1/2" with A Filter.
Plate 69(x): .16 1/5" with K2 Filter. Sun medium.
Plate 70(x): .16 1/10" with K2 Filter. Sun bright.
Plate 71(x): .16 1/10" with K2 Filter. Sun bright.
Plate 72(x): .16 1/10" with K2 Filter. Sun bright.
Plate 73: This picture is a collage made from portions of five separate photographs.
Plate 74: .16 1/10" with K2 Filter. Sun bright.
Plate 75: .16 3" Indirect daylight only. Sun bright outside. No filter.
Plate 76: .16 5", no filter. Ceiling light, one #2 photoflood, and indirect daylight.
Plate 77: .16 1/5" with K2 Filter. Sun bright.
Plate 78: Two exposures, each 1/10" at .16, no filter. In second exposure, figure moved out of picture.
Plate 79(x): .22 1/5" with K2 Filter. Sun bright.
Plate 80: .16 5", no filter. Indirect daylight only.
Plate 81: .16 1/10", no filter. Indirect daylight only.
Plate 82: .16 1/5" with K2 Filter. Sun medium.
Plate 83: .16 1/5" with K2 Filter. Sun medium.
Plate 84: .22 1/5" with K2 Filter. Sun bright.
Plate 85(x): .18 1/5" with K2 Filter. Sun bright.
Plate 86(x): .16 1/5" with K2 Filter. Sun bright, but mostly indirect.
Plate 87: .16 1/5" with K2 Filter. Sun bright, but mostly indirect.
Plate 88(x): .22 1/5" with K2 Filter. Sun bright.
Plate 89: .18 1/5" with K2 Filter. Sun bright.
Plate 90: .16 5", no filter. Indirect daylight only.
Plate 91: Double exposure. Exp. A: Plaster head set within opening in wall: .16 1/10", no filter.
Exp. B: same head, close-up: 6.3 1/10" using diffused daylight only, and throwing background out of focus.
Plate 92: .22 1" with K2 Filter. Indirect daylight.
Plate 93: .16 1/10" with K2 Filter. Sun bright, but getting low.
Plate 94: .16 1/10" with K2 Filter. Sun bright.
Plate 95: .16 1/5" with K2 Filter. Sun bright, but large shadow areas.
Plate 96: Double exposure. Exp. A: front of house: .22 1/10" with K2 Filter.
Exp. B: side of house, with model: .22 1/5" with K2 Filter.
Plate 97: .22 1/5" with K2 Filter. Sun medium.
Plate 98: Double exposure. Exp. A: close-up of fallen capital: .22 1/10" with K2 Filter.
Exp. B: .22 1/5" with K2 Filter.
Plate 99: This is a collage made from two separate photographs.
Plate 100: .16 1/5" with K2 Filter. Sun low and weak.
Note: In climates like that of Louisiana, all outside exposures must be somewhat heavier than might be expected because the high percentage of water vapor in the air acts to absorb, and scatter, light.